W0317079

cee

cee

CEE CEE
BERLIN

DISTANZ

CONTENTS

Berlin verkörpert auf eigenwillige Weise das 21. Jahrhundert. Für den anhaltenden Wandel und den Übergang vom analogen ins digitale Zeitalter ist die Stadt besonders gut gerüstet, musste sie sich in den letzten 110 Jahren doch ständig neu erfinden. Und das in raschem Tempo. Auf die Ära des Großbürgertums in der Kaiserzeit folgte der Erste Weltkrieg, die wilden Goldenen Zwanziger, die große Depression am Ende der Weimarer Republik; Naziregime und Zweiter Weltkrieg führten zur völligen Zerstörung. Es folgten der Wiederaufbau, die Teilung Deutschlands mit dem Bau der Mauer und schließlich 1989 ihr Fall.

Durch die Wiedervereinigung entstand in Berlin eine weltweit einmalige Situation: Die Stadtteile des ehemaligen Ostens wurden zu einem Labor für neue Ideen und Experimente. Es gab keine gesellschaftlichen Hierarchien, keinen Druck, der Wohnraum war billig und zog interessante und kreative Köpfe an, die sich hier in einem noch nicht definierten Umfeld frei entwickeln konnten.

Zuerst kamen die Künstler, dann die Entrepreneurs aus aller Welt. Aber es ging und geht immer um Ideen und die Herausforderung, wie man aus wenig etwas Neues schafft. Heute, 25 Jahre später, ist die Stadt eine riesige Baustelle. Überall entstehen neue Gebäude, Museen, Plätze – und vielleicht wird sogar irgendwann der internationale Flughafen eröffnet. So stelle ich mir den Bau von Babylon vor.

Sobald ein Stadtteil zu etabliert geworden ist, suchen sich die jungen Kreativen neue Ecken und Viertel, zum Arbeiten und Leben. Enthusiastisch und idealistisch verwirklichen sie ihre Projekte. Sie gründen Modelabels, eröffnen einen urbanen Garten, ein kleines Restaurant – oder starten ein digitales Projekt. So auch Nina Trippel und Sven Hausherr, die 2011 den Newsletter Cee Cee gegründet haben – eines meiner absoluten Lieblings-Blogs, das mein Leben und das vieler anderer wöchentlich aufs Neue bereichert und vergnüglicher macht.

Cee Cee ist ein kompetenter Guide durch die Flut an Eröffnungen – von Shops über Restaurants, Bars, Cafés bis hin zu kulturellen Events – in schön gestalteter Form. Jeden Donnerstag freue ich mich auf den neuen Newsletter mit vier bis sechs Tipps, darunter vielleicht ein neues Semifreddo-Eiscafé in Neukölln, ein koreanischer Imbiss in Kreuzberg oder ein am Vorabend eröffnetes Restaurant in Mitte. Alle Artikel sind ausgesprochen schön bebildert, sodass mir vor lauter Vorfreude das Wasser im Munde zusammenläuft, und die Texte anregend und angenehm knapp formuliert. Ich möchte nach Erhalt des neuesten Newsletters jedes Mal umgehend auf Entdeckungsreise gehen – und das tue ich auch!

Durch Cee Cee lerne ich jede Woche mindestens ein neues Geschäft oder Lokal in Berlin kennen. Da sich das kulturelle Leben in dieser Stadt seit einigen Jahren nicht mehr ausschließlich auf wenige Viertel konzentriert, ist es umso wichtiger geworden, einen zuverlässigen Wegweiser zu kennen. Deshalb musste dieses Best-of entstehen, das für jeden Berlinbewohner und -besucher unverzichtbar werden wird. Ich wünsche allen Lesern viele schöne Anregungen und Abenteuer mit diesem herrlichen Buch!

Ihre Berlin-Botschafterin,
Angelika Taschen

Berlin embodies the 21st century in a truly idiosyncratic manner. This city is especially well prepared for the constant change and transformation from the analogue into the digital world, since it has been forced to reinvent itself over and over throughout the last 110 years – at a rapid pace. After the era of the upper classes during the imperial period of World War I, the Golden and Roaring Twenties, the Great Depression hit Germany and ended the Weimar Republic. Nazi regime and World War II led to its complete destruction. Rebuilding and division of Germany followed with the construction of the Wall, until its ultimate fall in 1989.

Through Berlin's reunification, a truly unique situation came to life: districts in the former East became a laboratory for new ideas and experiments without social hierarchy or pressure. Residential spaces were cheap and attracted creative minds that could develop freely in the undefined environment; first came the artists, then entrepreneurs from all over the world followed suit. It was, and still is, about ideas and the challenges of creating something new from almost nothing. Today, 25 years later, the whole city is a big construction site: new buildings, museums, spots – and perhaps even the new airport may open one day. This is how I envision the construction of Babylon.

As soon as a district becomes established, the young creatives seek for new areas to live and work in. They realize their projects with enthusiasm and idealism. Some establish fashion labels, open up an urban garden or a small restaurant, or start a digital project: just like Nina Trippel and Sven Hausherr did, by introducing the Cee Cee newsletter in 2011 – one of my favorite digital reads, enriching and entertaining my life every week.

Cee Cee is a beautifully designed comprehensive guide through the flood of new openings of shops, restaurants, bars, cafes, and cultural events. Every Thursday I look forward to receiving the newsletter with four to six recommendations, perhaps with tips on a new semi-freddo ice cream parlor in Neukölln, a Korean eatery in Kreuzberg, or a Mitte-based restaurant that saw its opening just the night before. All articles are short yet articulate and motivating, often making my mouth water. Each and every time I receive the latest version, it makes me want to go on an expedition – and I actually do!

Through Cee Cee I learn of at least one new restaurant or shop in Berlin every week. Since the cultural life in this city doesn't exist in limited districts anymore, it has become even more important to have a reliable guide. That's why this best-of book had to be made, which will be essential for any residents and visitors. I wish all readers many wonderful inspirations and adventures with this gorgeous book.

Your Berlin ambassador,
Angelika Taschen

INDEX

INDEX

INDEX

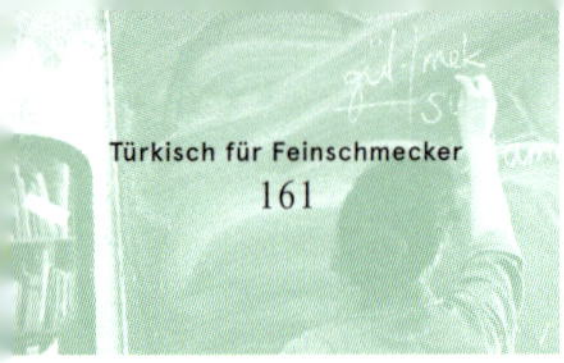

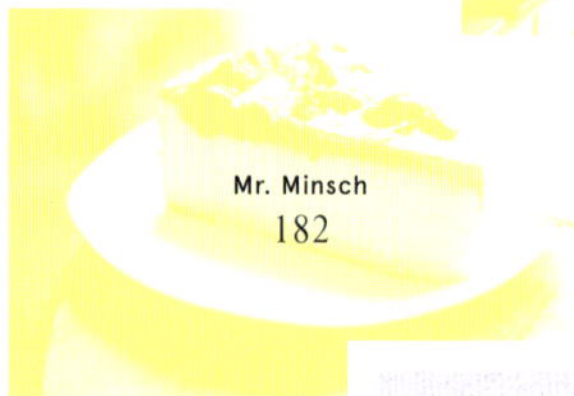

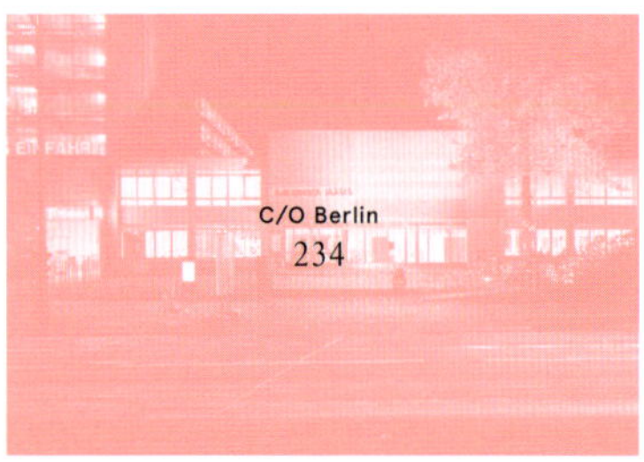

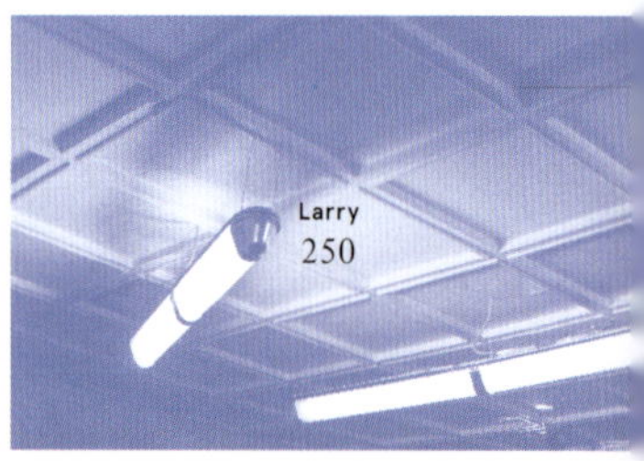

INDEX

HIDDEN GEMS

HINTER GRAUEN FASSADEN UND IN UNSCHEINBAREN HINTERHÖFEN VERSTECKT, WARTEN PERLEN DARAUF, ENTDECKT ZU WERDEN. EINMAL GESUCHT, FÜR IMMER GEFUNDEN. TUCKED BEHIND A BARELY MARKED DOOR, SECLUDED IN A COURTYARD, OR SIMPLY UPSTAIRS, THESE SPOTS MAY BE HARD TO FIND, BUT THAT MAKES THEM ALL THE MORE PRECIOUS.

MITTAGESSEN MIT ARCHITEKTEN
LUNCH WITH ARCHITECTS

Läge diese Kantine näher am Cee Cee-Office und Studio Hausherr, würden wir mehrmals pro Woche vorbeischauen. Hier kommt zusammen, was einen großartigen Lunch-Spot ausmacht: ein kleines, täglich wechselndes Menü mit drei Hauptgängen und Vorspeisen, faire Preise, schneller und zuvorkommender Service und nicht zu vergessen: das wunderschöne Interieur. Die Liebe zum Detail zeigt sich auch in dem formschönen Geschirr und Besteck. Kein Wunder, gehört die Kantine doch zum Berliner Büro von David Chipperfield Architects. Betrieben wird sie von der Crew des Restaurants Lokal (Linienstraße 160) – deshalb schmeckt das Essen hier wirklich lecker. We would be regulars at this cafeteria if it were located near Studio Hausherr and the Cee Cee office. It offers everything a good "lunch spot" should: a small daily menu with three main dishes and appetizers at great prices, fast and friendly staff, and beautiful, clean interior design with attention to even the most minute details down to the cutlery. Of course this comes as no surprise since the cafeteria is owned by the famous David Chipperfield Architects. And the food is delicious too, since the kitchen is operated by Lokal restaurant (Linienstraße 160). I shall travel the distance and return as often as possible.

Text & photos: Sven Hausherr

Chipperfield-Kantine
Joachimstraße 11, 10119 Berlin-Mitte
Mon-Fri 8:30-20:00, Lunch 12:00-15:00

Statt mit Architekten mit Schauspielern speisen? Das geht in der Kantine des Maxim Gorki Theaters in der Dorotheenstraße 9 in Mitte; die Terrasse ist wunderbar im Sommer. Want to have lunch with actors instead? Try Maxim Gorki's cafeteria at Dorotheenstraße 9 in Mitte; the garden terrace is truly lovely during summer.

Zum Dinner einfach die Straßenseite wechseln: Das Restaurant Richard in der Köpenicker Straße 174 in Kreuzberg ist eines der besten der Stadt. Cross the street for a special dinner: Restaurant Richard at Köpenicker Straße 174 in Kreuzberg is among the best in town.

FOTOKUNST IM MARMELADENLOFT
ART PHOTOGRAPHY IN A FORMER JAM FACTORY

Versteckt im Hinterhof einer alten Marmeladenfabrik in Kreuzberg befindet sich die Sammlung von Arthur de Ganay. Der französische Architekt und Sammler führt seit 2006 einmal im Monat persönlich durch sein Loft und zeigt nach Voranmeldung Privatschätze der deutschen und internationalen Fotokunst. Darunter sind große Namen der Becher-Schule wie Thomas Ruff und Candida Höfer. Die Arbeiten stehen hier nicht nur im Dialog zueinander, sondern interagieren auch mit dem einzigartigen Raum und der Spree, die durch die Fenster glitzert. Arthur de Ganay's photo collection is tucked away in the back alley of an old Art Nouveau jam factory in Kreuzberg. The French-born architect and collector has been giving monthly tours of his loft since 2006. He shows his incredible collection of German and international fine art photography, including big names from the Becher school like Thomas Ruff and Candida Höfer. In his unique exhibition space, with the Spree river sparkling beyond the windows, the large-scale works definitely resonate with one another.

Text: Laura Storfner

Fotografiesammlung Arthur de Ganay
Köpenicker Straße 10A, 10997 Berlin-Kreuzberg
Please note: Appointment via email is required
collectionarthurdeganay.com

Auf den Treppenstufen des Buchladens Pro qm in der Almstadtstraße 48–50 in Mitte blättern wir auch gerne – durch Publikationen von Politik bis Pop. Sit on the stairs in the Pro qm store at Almstadtstraße 48–50 in Mitte to browse through the books: everything from pop to politics.

DAS HINTERHOF-UNIVERSUM DER RARIÄTEN A COURTYARD UNIVERSE FULL OF RARITIES

Bevor ich das erste Mal bei Motto war, hatten mir schon dreizehn Freunde davon erzählt. Ich bin trotzdem fünfmal daran vorbeigelaufen. Nur das schnittige Logo über der Einfahrt verweist auf das Hinterhof-Geschäft von Alexis Zavialoff, in dem seit 2008 rund 4000 Publikationen auf knapp 40 Quadratmetern angeboten werden. Tritt man ein, glaubt man sich in der Buchhandlung aus Roman Polanskis „Die Neun Pforten" – allerdings mit weitaus zeitgenössischerem Material. Hier übertrumpft ein Buch das andere: Durchdachte Inhalte treffen auf schlüssige Gestaltung in Form von Künstlerportfolios, Ausstellungskatalogen oder moderner Lyrik. Neben dem hauseigenen Verlag und Vertrieb unterstützt Motto mit diversen Veranstaltungen unabhängige Künstler und Herausgeber. Die Stimmung ist beinahe familiär – spätestens, wenn die zufrieden schnurrende Hauskatze Tinte es sich neben einem bequem gemacht hat. Before finally finding this treasure trove of books and magazines, at least thirteen friends had mentioned this shop to me. Still, I walked past it five times. Now I know: look for the little snazzy sign above the courtyard entrance pointing to where Alexis Zavialoff houses around 4,000 publications in his 40-square-meter shop. Upon entering you feel like you're in Roman Polanski's "The Ninth Gate" – the only difference is that you're surrounded by contemporary publications. Here the books just keep getting more and more exciting, as sophisticated contents meet coherent designs – from artists' portfolios to exhibition catalogues to modern poetry. In addition to in-house publishing and distribution, Motto supports independent artists and editors with launches and events held at the shop. The atmosphere is cozy – even more so when the store cat Tinte is happily purring next to you.

Text: Max Winter / Photos: Benjamin Lindenkreuz

Motto
Skalitzer Straße 68, 10997 Berlin-Kreuzberg
Mon-Sat 12:00-20:00
mottodistribution.com

KAFFEE IM EHEMALIGEN PFÖRTNERHÄUSCHEN COFFEE IN A FORMER CONCIERGE HUT

Etwas versteckt in einem Hinterhof am Paul-Lincke-Ufer gibt es eine exzellente Station für Koffeinabhängige: Concierge Coffee. Aus der hohen Röstschule der Bonanza Coffee Heroes kommend, haben Benjamin Pates und sein Partner Namy Nosratifard im August 2013 hier ihrer Vision eines Cafés Leben eingehaucht. Concierge Coffee ist so charmant wie speziell, denn eigentlich ist es nur ein kleines Pförtnerhäuschen. Aber auf knapp 15 Quadratmetern ist genug Platz für richtig guten Kaffee. Die Empfehlung des Hauses: ein gepflegter Flat White. Zum Genießen vor Ort und natürlich zum Mitnehmen. Hidden in a backyard on Paul-Lincke-Ufer, a small café welcomes caffeine junkies: Concierge Coffee. The boys, Benjamin Pates and his partner Namy Nosratifard, are protégés of Berlin's famous café and roastery, Bonanza Coffee Heroes. They turned a former concierge hut into their vision of a perfect petit café: a mere 15-square-meter space with a window to sell their excellent coffee. What they're lacking in size, they make up for in aroma and flavor. I always go for the house recommendation: a perfect flat white - to be enjoyed on site or on the go.

Text: Astrid Bruckmann / Photos: Marta Greber, Namy Nosratifard

Concierge Coffee
Paul-Lincke-Ufer 39-40, 10999 Berlin-Kreuzberg
Mon-Fri 8:30-18:00, Sat 12:00-17:00

Auch bei den Nachbarn vorbeischauen: hervorragende und authentische japanische Nudelsupppen gibt's gleich nebenan bei Cocolo Ramen, am Paul-Lincke-Ufer 39. Cocolo Ramen – just next door – at Paul-Lincke-Ufer 39 is a heavenly spot for authentic Japanese cuisine.

KLEINE RÄUME FÜR GROSSE KUNST A SMALL STAGE FOR GREAT ART

Wolfgang Tillmans ist nicht nur einer der bekanntesten Fotografen und Künstler, sondern auch Ausstellungsmacher. Seit 2006 betreibt er den nicht-kommerziellen Kunstraum Between Bridges - zunächst in London und seit Anfang 2014 in Schöneberg. Auf 50 überschaubaren Quadratmetern präsentiert Tillmans Etabliertes, Unbekanntes und Wiederentdecktes aus allen Disziplinen und ergreift mit seinem Projektraum die Chance, Werke unabhängig vom Markt zu zeigen. Ein versteckter Ort für Kunst, den es zu besuchen lohnt. Wolfgang Tillmans is not only one of the most famous German artists and fine-art photographers, but he is also a curator. Since 2006 he's been running a non-commercial art space called Between Bridges, which moved from London to Berlin's Schöneberg in 2014. In his 50-square-meter space, Tillmans presents established, unknown, and rediscovered artwork from all disciplines by openly embracing his independence from the art market. An unassuming location for inspiring art that is worth discovering.

Text: Mathis Neuhaus

Between Bridges
Keithstraße 15, 10787 Berlin-Schöneberg
Wed-Sat 12:00-18:00
betweenbridges.net

CEE CEE'S GUEST: KIRSTEN HERMANN

Als Kirsten Hermann 2003 nach Berlin zog, war Mitte noch ein anderes Pflaster. Das italienische Restaurant Bruno, Heinz' und Inges Alt Berlin, der legendäre Schuhladen Calypso – inzwischen alle nicht mehr da. „Ich bin nicht sentimental, Dinge verändern sich und das sollen sie auch", sagt sie und ist selbst weitergezogen. Privat und beruflich: von der Alten Schönhauser Straße in die Schröderstraße, eine ruhige Seitenstraße. Aber wenn Kirsten zum Opening in die Galerie für Moderne Fotografie lädt, ist es vorbei mit der Beschaulichkeit – dann bildet sich ein großer Pulk auf dem Bürgersteig. Kein Wunder, besteht ihre 2008 eröffnete Galerie doch nur aus einem kleinen Raum, und so versammelt sich das Publikum eben draußen. Genug Platz für Einzel- und Gruppenausstellungen bietet sie aber trotzdem: Ob Stillleben von Ingar Krauss oder historische DDR-Modefotos von Roger Melis – Kirsten legt sich stilistisch nicht fest, beweist aber stets ein Auge für das Außergewöhnliche. Abstand vom Trubel und Berlin an sich findet sie auf Landpartien. Und im Winter? „Fahr so lange wie möglich in die Sonne", rät sie – hat aber eine innerstädtische Alltagsflucht gen Süden in petto: Das Fischrestaurant Balikci Ergün. When Kirsten Hermann moved to Berlin in 2003, Mitte was a completely different place. Bruno's Italian restaurant, Heinz & Inge's pub Alt Berlin, the legendary shoe store Calypso – they have all left. Kirsten, however, claims that she is not sentimental: "Things change and they should." She has since moved on herself, both in her private and professional life from Alte Schönhauser Straße to Schröderstraße, off the beaten path. Tranquility quickly comes to an end, however, when her gallery has opening nights. Galerie für Moderne Fotografie opened in 2008 and only consists of a small room, but attracts large art-loving crowds, who are more than happy to block the sidewalk and mingle outside. But most importantly, the space offers enough room for solo and group exhibitions. Whether it is still life images by Ingar Krauss or historic GDR fashion photographs by Roger Melis, Kirsten does not commit to a particular style. Nonetheless, she always has an eye for the extraordinary. To relax from her hectic Berlin work life, she escapes to the countryside. In order to survive winter, she advises to "go on vacation somewhere sunny for as long as possible." But she also has a tip for an inner-city escape: the fish restaurant Balikci Ergün. →

Galerie für Moderne Fotografie, Schröder Straße 13, 10115 Berlin-Mitte
galeriefuermodernefotografie.com

KIRSTEN HERMANN EMPFIEHLT: BALIKCI ERGÜN

KIRSTEN HERMANN RECOMMENDS: BALIKCI ERGÜN

Das Balikci Ergün in den S-Bahnbögen nahe der Station Bellevue ist eigentlich ein Fischhandel und war zunächst ein illegales Restaurant. Draußen sitzt man wie in einer Gartenkolonie und schaut auf die bizarren Wohnungen der Bundestagsabgeordneten. Innen ist es wie im Urlaub in der Türkei – oder zumindest nicht wie in Berlin. Das Schöne: deutscher Fleiß und Korrektheit bleiben draußen, und spontane Musik gehört hier genauso zum Leben wie der hervorragende und frische Fisch, der immer montags und freitags geliefert wird. Gekocht und serviert wird er von einer richtigen Familienbande. Von der Decke raschelt ein Kartenwald, beschrieben mit Liebeserklärungen an dieses kleine Stück Türkei mitten in Berlin – so nah und doch so fern von Schloss Bellevue und der großen Politik. Located under the S-Bahn arches near the Bellevue station, Balikci Ergün, which started out as an illegal restaurant, is actually a fishmonger. Outside it feels like you are seated in one of Berlin's garden colonies; the only difference is the view on the German parliament members' bizarre apartments. Inside you feel like you're on a vacation in Turkey or at least somewhere far away. That's what's so great about this place – not only are you spared German assiduity and correctness, but spontaneous music is revered as something important in life. Their superb and fresh fish is delivered on Mondays and Fridays, and prepared and served by the huge family. Rustling paper clouds with handwritten declarations of love to this tiny piece of Turkey in the heart of Berlin hang from the ceiling – so close yet so far away from Bellevue Castle and the world of politics.

Text: Kirsten Hermann / Photos: Marta Greber

<ins>Balikci Ergün</ins>
Lüneburger Straße 382, 10557 Berlin-Moabit
Daily 15:00-24:00

Seit es Shiso Burger in der Auguststraße 29 in Mitte gibt, sind Burgerketten bei Kirstens Teenagertochter Puki total out. Thanks to Shiso Burger at Auguststraße 29 in Mitte, fast food chains are outdated – even for Kirsten's teenage daughter Puki.

KUNSTFÜHRUNGEN AUF DEM EX-STASI-AREAL ART TOURS IN A FORMER STASI AREA

Zum Alexanderplatz dauert es acht Minuten, doch zwischen Herzbergstraße und Fernsehturm liegen Welten: Graffiti, Brachland und das Dong Xuan Center. Vor mehr als 20 Jahren befand sich hier die Hochsicherheitszone der DDR, wo der frühere Fahrdienst des Zentralkomitees der SED hohen Besuch aus dem Westen empfing. Heute findet man auf 18.000 Quadratmetern neben KFZ-Werkstätten und Schreinereien auch haubrokprojects – die Sammlung von Axel und Barbara Haubrok. In geschichtsträchtiger Umgebung, zwischen intakter Kegelbahn und Sauna, zeigt das Paar Werke von Konzeptkunst bis Minimal Art. Deep in Berlin-Lichtenberg, now a graffiti wasteland, the GDR had its maximum security zone. This is where the former Socialist Unity Party of Germany (SED) received its high-ranking visitors from the West over 20 years ago. The 18,000 square meters of land has since been converted into a space for auto repair shops and carpentry workshops. And recently, the grounds saw the addition of the haubrokprojects, an art collection owned by Axel and Barbara Haubrok. Upon request, the couple will guide you through their collection of conceptual and minimal art pieces.

Text: Laura Storfner / Photos: Ludger Paffrath

haubrokprojects
Fahrbereitschaft, Herzbergstraße 40-43, 10365 Berlin-Lichtenberg
By appointment only
haubrok.org

KLASSIK IN INDUSTRIELLEM AMBIENTE CLASSICAL MUSIC IN AN INDUSTRIAL AMBIANCE

Im Stil der Pariser Institutionen Maison Erard oder Salle Pleyel aus dem 19. Jahrhundert verwandelt sich gegen Abend mitten im Wedding eine Werkstatt für historische Flügel in einen Pianosalon. Der Raum ist spärlich durch einige Schirmlampen erhellt, Industrieleuchten werfen einen Lichtkegel in die Mitte der Halle. Es wird geraucht, Wein getrunken, gefachsimpelt. Die Atmosphäre ist unprätentiös und gemütlich. Der Blick fällt immer wieder auf die unzähligen Klaviere, die kreuz und quer im Raum verteilt sind. Sobald das Konzert beginnt, wird es still und auf der „Bühne" spielen bei meinem Besuch Itamar Zorman auf der Violine und Julien Quentin am Klavier Werke von Tschaikowsky, Ravel und Brahms. Die eingeladenen Künstler gehören zur Weltspitze der klassischen Musik – ich bin beeindruckt und erlebe einen Abend, der noch lange nachhallt. From time to time, in the style of the Parisian Maison Erard or Salle Pleyel from the 19th century, an industrial workshop for historical pianos in the middle of Wedding turns into Piano Salon Christophori. The room is dimly lit with old shaded lamps. Industrial lights cast a beam of light in the middle of the hall, where the musicians perform. Before the concert commences, the audience of around 200 people chats, smokes, and drinks wine, but once the musicians appear, silence takes over the room. The performers on "stage" are some of the world's best classical musicians; when I visited the piano salon, it was Itamar Zorman on violin and Julien Quentin on piano, playing works by Tchaikovsky, Ravel, and Brahms. I was truly impressed and the evening's memory shall be treasured forever.

Text & photos: Martin Mascheski

Piano Salon Christophori
Uferstraße 8, 13357 Berlin-Wedding
Sign up online in advance to attend. Your kind 14 Euro donation includes free drinks.
konzertfluegel.com

OUT OF
THE BOX
INTO

DAS SHOPPING-APARTMENT ODER: ZUHAUSE BEI BLESS

TO SHOP OR TO STAY: THE BLESS APARTMENT STORE

Man muss klingeln, um Einlass in diese Prenzlberger Hinterhofwohnung gewährt zu bekommen. Geöffnet wird die Tür bei BLESS HOME BERLIN von wechselnden Personen, die das Shop-Apartment vorübergehend bewohnen. Ein Besuch ist daher eine intime Angelegenheit: Man darf durch Schlaf- und Wohnzimmer wandeln oder auf den Balkon treten und sich Zeit nehmen mit der Frage, ob eine Hängematte aus Pelz oder lieber ein rollendes Tablett das eigene Leben aufwerten könnten. Von der Decke hängen die aktuelle Kollektion, Einzelstücke und sogar Archivteile, die es sonst nicht mehr zu kaufen gibt, weil sie nur noch einmal existieren. Auf Anfrage kann man hier sogar übernachten. Wenn das kein Traum ist?! You have to ring the bell and climb the stairs to enter this shop-apartment located in a Prenzlauer Berg courtyard. The temporary resident there will greet you at the door and guide you through BLESS HOME BERLIN. This is a truly intimate shopping experience. Take your time as you walk through the bedroom and kitchen, and contemplate whether the furry hammock or knitted shoes would be the best addition to your life. Clothes from BLESS' current collection hang from the ceiling as well as classics and archive pieces you won't find anywhere else. Their opening hours are very limited, but don't fret, you can even request to stay overnight. To all BLESS fans: isn't this a dream come true?

Text: Nina Trippel / Photos: Tim Schroeder, Ludger Paffrath

Eine der jüngsten aber besten Bars der Gegend: Kapitalist in der Oderberger Straße 2 – Cash nicht vergessen! Among the newly opened bars in this area, our favorite is Kapitalist at Oderberger Straße 2 – don't forget to bring cash!

BLESS SHOP / HOME BERLIN
Oderberger Straße 60, backhouse, 3rd floor
10435 Berlin-Prenzlauer Berg
Mon 10:00-12:00, Wed-Sun 15:00-20:00 & by appointment
bless-service.de

EISTEE & CHAI AUS DER HINTERHOFMANUFAKTUR HOMEMADE ICED TEA & CHAI BLENDS

Angefangen hat alles mit ein paar Flaschen Eistee: minimal süß, aber mit einem Maximum an Geschmack. Mit Liebe und Leidenschaft im Berliner Hinterhof gebraut – in der ManuTeeFaktur. Im Jahr 2012 verkaufte Manu Kumar seine liebevoll gestalteten Flaschen noch nebenbei. Seine Kreationen sind jedoch wahre Erfolgsrezepte, was zu einer erhöhten Nachfrage und Sortimentserweiterung geführt hat: Neben dem Tuareg Mint Tea auf Grüntee-Basis, mit Limette und Himalaya-Kristallsalz verfeinert, und dem vietnamesisch inspirierten Lemongrass-Tea gibt es inzwischen auch klassischen schwarzen Tee aus Indien und Sri Lanka. Die intensiven Mischungen in kleinen Gläsern – wie der Kahwah Kashmiri mit Rosenblättern, den man im Norden Indiens gerne nach dem Essen trinkt – sind auch schöne Gastgeschenke für Freunde. Seine Lieferanten kennt Manu alle persönlich und regionale Zutaten, wie Minze, werden von ihm selbst verlesen. Überhaupt macht er alles im wahrsten Sinne des Wortes eigenhändig, und wenn man ihn besucht, kann man durch die Scheibe in die Küche linsen und bei einer Tasse Tee verweilen. Also Zeit vor Ort einplanen und sich danach mit einem Eistee ans Kanalufer setzen. Dann ist der Weg nicht weit – für den Nachschub. Hand-brewed in a courtyard in Kreuzberg with passion and dedication, this local tea brand has become a recent Berlin favorite. The iced tea is one of the best we've tasted: the refreshing varieties are slightly sweet, and brewed to achieve maximum flavor. Founded in 2012 by Manu Kumar, this bottled tea brand quickly became his full-time occupation. The Tuareg Mint Tea, a green tea combined with lime and Himalayan crystal salt, and the Vietnamese-inspired Lemongrass Tea with kaffir leaves are the two classics. Traditional black teas now complete the range. Packed in little glass jars, his intense chai tea such as Kahwah Kashmiri with rose petals, a common after-dinner drink in northern India, makes a great gift for friends. Manu knows all his suppliers and checks their regional produce regularly, and he's often at the store, making the tea himself. Sneak a peek into his kitchen, enjoy a cup of tea, and a little chat. Then pick up a bottle of iced tea to enjoy by the canal. But don't go too far – you'll certainly want another one.

Text: Nina Trippel / Photos: Ira Hadžić, Manu Kumar

ManuTeeFaktur
Paul-Lincke-Ufer 44A, 2nd courtyard building, 10999 Berlin-Kreuzberg
Mon-Sat, open when open
manuteefaktur.com

Fans von japanischem Grüntee und Matcha schauen im Berliner Onlineshop sunday.de vorbei. Green tea and matcha aficionados can browse through the Berlin-based online store sunday.de

DIE KLEINE OASE IN RIXDORF
A SMALL OASIS IN RIXDORF

So hätte sich das Comenius, der Pädagoge aus dem 17. Jahrhundert, bestimmt gewünscht: Ein Garten für Groß und Klein inmitten des Böhmischen Dorfes, ganz nach seiner Vorstellung „Alle alles in Rücksicht auf das Ganze zu lehren". Und wo sonst könnte man das große Ganze besser verstehen als in der Natur? Ein schmaler Pfad führt vorbei an einer Steinmauer und Obstbäumen, einer hölzernen Bühne, hin zum sogenannten Seelenparadies – einem Pavillon mit perfektem Blick aufs „Weltenmeer". Vorbei an einem kleinen Teich in unmittelbarer Nähe zum Irrgarten, zum Arzneigärtlein und dem Mosaischen Becken. Das klingt nach einer gigantischen Anlage, die einen mit ihrer Geschichte erschlägt. Doch weit gefehlt: Dieser Garten ist klein, erfreulich unaufdringlich und wunderschön anzusehen. Perfekt für einen sonnigen Nachmittag und versteckt im hektischen Neukölln. Ein charmanter Ruhepol. Um hineinzugelangen muss man den auf der Rückseite des Gatters befindlichen kleinen Summer drücken. The pedagog Comenius from the 17th century would have been pleased. A garden in the heart of the Bohemian village of Rixdorf in Neukölln, a place to meet for young and old alike, is the perfect spot to visualize his motto "Teach everything to everyone in a holistic manner." And what's a better place to see the big picture than in nature? A little pathway leads you through the garden. You'll pass a brick wall, fruit trees, and a wooden stage named after Comenius' book "School by Play" ("Schola Ludus"). Further on, you'll pass a "Paradise for Souls" ("Seelenparadies"), a pavilion offering a perfect view of the "Earth's Sea" ("Weltenmeer"). There's also a little pond next to a labyrinth. It might sound like this history-infused ground is huge, but don't worry, it's actually a small, charming garden that's simply beautiful to stroll through on a sunny afternoon. To enter, press the little button behind the gate.

Text & photos: Martin Mascheski

Comenius-Garten
Richardstraße 35, 12043 Berlin-Neukölln

Danach lohnt ein Bummel entlang der Richardstraße bis zur Hausnummer 103 – für eine Stärkung bei Zsa Zsa & Loui.
For sandwiches and snacks, walk down Richardstraße until your reach Zsa Zsa & Loui at house number 103.

Zum Abendessen ins Da Baffi in der Nazarethkirchstraße 41 in Wedding: Hier werden Pulpo-Carpaccio und frischer Trüffel serviert sowie Weine, die direkt vom Winzer kommen. For dinner, head to Da Baffi at Nazarethkirchstraße 41 in Wedding for pulpo (octopus) carpaccio, fresh truffles, and wines that come directly from the vintners.

ITALIENISCHES AM SCHLESI
ITALIAN BITES NEAR SCHLESI

Das Da Baffi – für uns der beste Italiener im Wedding – hat seit 2013 eine kleine Schwester in Kreuzberg: Die Salumeria Lamuri bietet Frühstück, Mittagessen, Kaffee und verschiedene Aperitife in atemberaubendem Interieur. Kaum zu glauben, dass dieses Schmuckstück mit seinen schönen Bodenfliesen, der verzierten Decke und den Wandmalereien früher ein Elektrogeschäft war. Das Lamuri ist ideal zum Mittagessen, denn serviert wird einfache, aber köstliche italienische Küche: Salate oder Pasta – natürlich alles hausgemacht mit besten Zutaten. Die Panini, Antipasti und Weine sowie die eigens zubereiteten Saucen kann man auch mitnehmen, wenn man sich ein wenig Da Baffi- und Lamuri-Atmosphäre in die eigene Küche zaubern möchte. Da Baffi, an Italian restaurant in Wedding, just opened up a little sister joint in Kreuzberg. Salumeria Lamuri is only open during the day, offering breakfast, lunch, coffees, and aperitifs in a stunning environment. It is hard to believe that this gem of a place, with its beautiful floor tiles, ornamented ceilings, and wall paintings, once housed an electrical store. Lamuri is perfect for lunch, serving simple yet delicious Italian cuisine all made with high-quality ingredients. You can also purchase some of their great wines, antipasti, and homemade sauces, so you can take a little piece of Da Baffi and Lamuri home with you.

Text: Sven Hausherr / Photos: Marta Greber, Ana Santl

Salumeria Lamuri
Köpenicker Straße 183, 10997 Berlin-Kreuzberg
Mon-Fri 9:00-18:00, Sat 10:00-18:00
lasalumeria.wordpress.com

BO RDE RL ESS

VON SCHWEDISCHEM GEBÄCK BIS ZU KOREANISCHEM STREET FOOD – BERLIN WIRD JEDEN TAG EIN WENIG INTERNATIONALER. WIR NEHMEN GERNE EINE KOSTPROBE. BERLIN BECOMES MORE AND MORE INTERNATIONAL EVERYDAY, ESPECIALLY THE FOOD SCENE. FROM SWEDISH PASTRIES TO KOREAN STREET FOOD – TASTE THE WORLD OUTSIDE YOUR DOOR.

TEXTILHANDWERK AUS ALLER WELT ETHNIC TEXTILES FROM ACROSS THE GLOBE

International Wardrobe – das hört sich nach Kleidung an, die man überall tragen kann. Und so ist es auch: Katharina Koppenwallner sorgt dafür. Sie spürt Trachten und ethnische Textilarbeiten aus aller Herren Länder auf und zeigt sie der großen, weiten Welt. Ob Ikat-Seidenschals der Khmer aus Kambodscha oder handbestickte Kissen aus Kalotaszeg – einer von Ungarn bewohnten Region im Nordwesten Transsilvaniens –, jedes Stück erzählt von seiner Herkunft und Herstellungsweise. Textile Völkerverständigung sozusagen. Katharina Koppenwallner finds unique and striking textiles, often made using archaic techniques: one-of-a-kind, handmade pieces from remote places. She resells them at International Wardrobe in order to share these treasures with the world – the history behind each piece along with the stories of the people who make them. Jackets and pillows from Kalotaszeg, a region in northern Transylvania inhabited by Hungarians, blouses from the Bukovina, or Ikat silk scarves from Cambodia. Visit the shop and travel the world through textiles.

Text: Nina Trippel / Photos: Chloé Richard, Fred Dott

International Wardrobe
Almstadtstraße 50, 10119 Berlin-Mitte
Mon-Wed by appointment, Thu-Sat 12:00-19:00

Für brasilianisch-italienisches Flair und Kieztalk: auf einen Açai-Smoothie oder einen Espresso geht man zu Nea ins Buscaglione in der Rochstraße 3, ganz in der Nähe.
For Brazilian-Italian flair and some neighborhood gossip: visit Nea nearby at Buscaglione at Rochstraße 3 for a glass of Açai juice or an espresso.

Apropos Mid-Century-Modern und Skandinavien: Bei Vintage Galore nebenan gibt es eine wunderbare Auswahl an Möbeln für das eigene Zuhause. Speaking of mid-century modernism and Scandinavia: Next door, at Vintage Galore, there is a wonderful selection of furniture for your home.

SMÖRGÅSBORD SKANDINAVISCHER KÖSTLICHKEITEN SMORGASBORD OF SCANDINAVIAN DELIGHTS

Bunte Blumensträuße auf Mid-Century-Möbeln, eine Theke aus Holzplanken und vor allem die Gastgeberin selbst versprühen hier jede Menge skandinavischen Charme. Wer in dieser Atmosphäre nur den köstlichen Kaffee genießt, verpasst die kulinarischen Highlights: Hinter Smørrebrød, zu deutsch Butterbrot, verbirgt sich nämlich weit mehr als der Name vermuten lässt. Und als Vegetarierin ist Inhaberin Lo ohnehin stets um Abwechslung bemüht. Angeboten wird deshalb nicht nur das klassische Smørrebrød, sondern auch Feigenbrot – mit allerlei Beeren, Nüssen, Salat und Käse belegt. Neben Blumen pflückt die Inhaberin in den Treptower Gärten auch einen Teil der frischen Zutaten. Überraschen lassen kann man sich von dem ständig wechselnden Angebot an Gebäck: nach Zimt duftende Kanelbullar, pastellfarbene Prinsesstårta, Mandel- oder Blaubeerkuchen. Colorful bouquets placed on mid-century furniture, a desk made of wooden planks, and a charming hostess add loads of special Scandinavian feel to Café Valentin. But if all you do is drink their delicious coffee, you will miss the real culinary highlights. Behind Smørrebrød (buttered bread) is much more to discover than the name suggests. Being a vegetarian, the café's owner Lo is always seeking to refresh her menu. Thus, next to their classics, she also sells fig bread topped and stuffed with all kinds of berries, nuts, salads, and cheese. Lo doesn't just pick the flowers from Treptow's gardens herself, some parts of her fresh ingredients are also from there. Let yourself be pleasantly surprised by the ever-changing selection of her pastries: cinnamon scented Kanelbullar, pastel Prinsesstårta, and almond and blueberry cakes.

Text & photos: Anna-Maria Scharf

Café Valentin
Sanderstraße 13, 12047 Berlin-Neukölln
Mon 11:00-18:00, Tue 11:00-15:00, Wed-Sun 11:00-18:00

CEE CEE'S GUEST: JANA GUMPRECHT

Oft ist sie nicht in Berlin, aber wenn, dann richtig: Dann wird Jana Gumprechts Dachterrasse mit Blick auf den Fernsehturm und die Hohenschönhausener Plattenbauten zur erweiterten Dinner-Location und der Tisch reichhaltig gedeckt. Wie man zu Janas legendären Essen eingeladen wird? Jemanden kennen, der jemanden kennt, der eingeladen ist – und mitkommen. Und „vorher einfach bei Goldhahn & Sampson (Dunckerstraße 9) einen guten Schampus einpacken", sagt Jana. „Bei deren Auswahl kann man nämlich keine Fehler machen." Die zuvorkommende und trotzdem entspannte Gastgeberin zu mimen, scheint ihr keine Mühe zu bereiten. Die Nacht bis zum Morgen zu zelebrieren ebenso wenig. Könnte berufsbedingt sein – als Stylistin und Modefotografin reist sie ständig bis ans andere Ende der Welt und setzt Models für Werbeaufnahmen und Editorials in Szene. Kaum zurück in Berlin, sehnt sie sich gleich wieder nach einer kosmopolitischen Dosis. Janas ganz persönlicher Tipp für internationalen Gaumenkitzel ist ein japanisches Kleinod, das sie direkt nach der Eröffnung entdeckt hat: Nazuna.

She doesn't spend much time in Berlin, but when she does, she knows how to work the city: her rooftop terrace, which overlooks Berlin's famous TV tower and the high-rise blocks of Hohenschönhausen, turns into a dinner venue with tables laden with gorgeous food. How does one get invited to her legendary dinner parties? If you know someone who knows someone who is invited – tag along. And "just pick up a good bubbly at Goldhahn & Sampson (Dunckerstraße 9)," says Jana. "You can't go wrong with their selection." She's the ideal hostess, celebrating from dusk till dawn. Her worldliness can be traced directly to her profession – as a stylist and fashion photographer, she travels around the world working with models on commercials and editorial productions. The moment she returns to Berlin, she needs her shot of cosmopolitan life and inspiration. Jana's personal tip when craving something international: Nazuna, a paradise for lovers of Japanese sweets, which she discovered shortly after its opening. →

JANA GUMPRECHT EMPFIEHLT: NAZUNA JANA GUMPRECHT RECOMMENDS: NAZUNA

Seit 2011 gibt diesen schönen, geradlinigen Laden in der Danziger Straße – ein Zufluchtsort für Menschen wie mich, die über jede Art ehrlicher und professionell umgesetzter kulinarischer Vision in Prenzlauer Berg hocherfreut sind. Tsuki Hasegawa, japanische Spezialitäten-Köchin, und Sven Schumacher, Patissier, bieten hier leckere japanische Kleinigkeiten, Bento-Boxen, Salate mit originellen Dressings, Reis-Seetang-Snacks und natürlich Süßes an: herrliche Reiskuchen, Törtchen, Desserts und Schokoladen mit Bohnenmus, Matcha & Co – fein abgeschmeckt und mit großer Liebe zum Detail zubereitet. Dazu gibt es japanische Tees, zu allen Kreationen ein Lächeln und immer eine kleine Geschichte oder Erklärung – da gerät man ins Schwelgen und hat die Qual der Wahl. Es hilft nichts: Man muss einfach oft hingehen! After many days of waiting and searching, a place for people who appreciate professional and honest culinary visions has finally opened in Prenzlauer Berg in 2011. The Japanese chef, Tsuki Hasegawa, offers beautiful, tasty Japanese morsels such as bento boxes, salads with exquisite and inventive dressings, and classic rice balls wrapped in nori seaweed. Sven Schumacher, the pâtissier, presents superb sweets such as rice cakes, tartlets, chocolate with bean paste, matcha, and many more. Everything is created with a great love for detail. Additionally, there are Japanese teas and a lovely smile with anecdotes about the food and its origin.

Text: Jana Gumprecht / Photos: Edisonga

Nazuna
Danziger Straße 65, 10435 Berlin-Prenzlauer Berg
Tue-Fri 12:00-20:00, Sat 12:00-18:00
nazuna-berlin.com

In Vintage-Stimmung? Bei Das Neue Schwarz in der Mulackstraße 38, im Herzen von Mitte, wird man immer fündig. In a vintage mood? You can get lucky in Das Neue Schwarz at Mulackstraße 38 in the heart of Mitte.

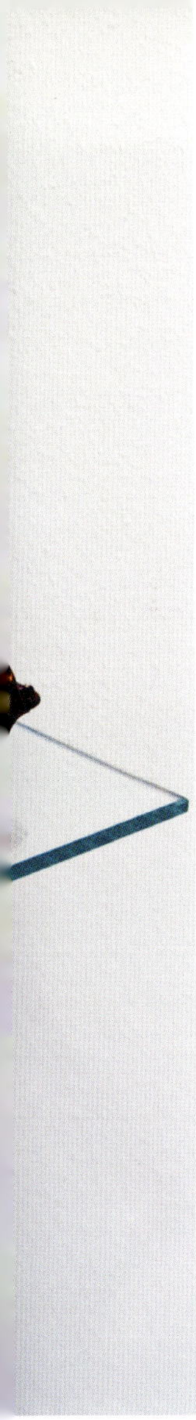

UM DIE WELT MIT VINTAGE-MODE
AROUND THE WORLD WITH VINTAGE FASHION

„I'm in love with cities I've never been to", steht auf dem kleinen Schaufenster in der Linienstraße, das zum Vintage-Shop Townes gehört. Von hier aus kann man auch ohne Flugticket einen Blick in die Schränke dieser Welt werfen. "Wir reisen über unsere Kleidung; besondere Stücke entführen uns an fremde Orte und in eine andere Zeit", beschreibt Inhaberin Shoko Kawaida das Konzept. Sie selbst ist viel unterwegs - ursprünglich aus Tokio, hat sie bereits in Arkansas, Amsterdam und Paris gelebt, als Designerin gearbeitet und ihre Modeschätze schließlich nach Berlin gebracht. Auf wenigen Quadratmetern finden Männer und Frauen deshalb kein typisches Secondhand-Sortiment, sondern internationale High Fashion aus verschiedenen Epochen: Röcke von Comme des Garçons aus den späten Siebzigern, Jacken von Helmut Lang aus den Neunzigern oder Taschen von Céline. Jedes Kleidungsstück hat seine eigene, kleine Geschichte, und die wunderbare Inhaberin erzählt sie gerne. A small shop window on Linienstraße says: "I'm in love with cities I've never been to." It's at Townes, a vintage shop that offers a journey around the world without having to leave Berlin. "We travel through our garments. Special pieces take us to different places and times," says shop owner Shoko Kawaida, describing the store concept. Originally from Tokyo, Shoko has traveled to many places and lived in many parts of the world, including Arkansas, Amsterdam, and Paris, where she worked as a designer before moving to Berlin with heaps of fashion treasures. Her tiny boutique stocks rare pieces by international designers: Comme des Garçon's early pieces from the late seventies, jackets by Helmut Lang, and bags by Céline. All items are connected to her travels and the lovely owner will gladly share her stories with you.

Text: Laura Storfner / Photos: Benjamin Lindenkreuz

Townes
Linienstraße 56, 10119 Berlin-Mitte
Mon-Sat 12:00-20:00

DER KOSMOPOLIT UNTER DEN AUSSTELLUNGSHÄUSERN

THE COSMOPOLITAN ART SPACE

Das Haus der Kulturen der Welt (HKW) inmitten des Regierungsviertels ist ein Multitalent. Es bietet Kunstinteressierten eine Plattform für Diskurse und ein Programm, das über konventionelle Ausstellungen hinausgeht und besonders nichteuropäische Kulturen in den Fokus rückt. Außerdem ist die Kongresshalle, die sogenannte Schwangere Auster von Hugh Stubbins (Assistent von Bauhaus-Gründer Walter Gropius), für Architekturfreunde ein Muss, da sie 1957 zur Internationalen Bauausstellung Interbau errichtet wurde – einer Zeit, in der auch viele Häuser im nahe gelegenen Hansaviertel entstanden. Das Ausstellungsprogramm wird im Sommer auf der riesigen Terrasse fortgeführt – als Open-Air-Kino oder Konzertbühne. Hier kann man mit Blick auf die Spree aber auch einfach die Seele baumeln lassen. The Haus der Kulturen der Welt, located in the middle of the government district, is a multifaceted space. With a clear focus on non-European cultures, it offers art enthusiasts a platform for discourse and sophisticated programs that surpass conventional exhibitions. Moreover, the building designed by Hugh Stubbins (a former assistant to Walter Gropius, founder of the Bauhaus) is a must for friends of architecture, because it was constructed during the 1957 International Building Exhibition or "Interbau"; a time when many of the famous buildings in the nearby Hansaviertel were built. During the summer, the programs at "the pregnant oyster," as locals like to call it, continue in the huge outdoor area in the form of concerts or open air cinema. The view of the Spree River makes it a great place to hang out and relax, too.

Text: Mathis Neuhaus / Photos: Mila Hacke

Haus der Kulturen der Welt
John-Foster-Dulles-Allee 10, 10557 Berlin-Tiergarten
Daily 10:00-19:00, Exhibitions: Wed-Mon 11:00-19:00
hkw.de

Wer ein Ziel braucht, um den Tiergarten zu durchqueren: Die Nordischen Botschaften in der Rauchstraße 1 locken wochentags ab 13 Uhr mit einem leckerem Lunch. If you need a reason to cross Tiergarten Park, The Nordic Embassies offer great lunches on weekdays from 1 a.m. at Rauchstraße 1.

ZUM PICKNICK NACH THAILAND
A WEEKEND TRIP TO THAILAND

Jedes Wochenende trifft sich die Berliner Thai-Community im Preußenpark in Wilmersdorf, mittlerweile besser als Thai-Park bekannt. Auf zahllosen Decken und Matten werden mobile Mini-Küchen aufgebaut und frische, leckere und vor allem authentische Gerichte zubereitet – man sollte gegebenenfalls erwähnen, dass man es nicht zu scharf möchte ... Unbedingt auch den Thai-Eistee und die tennisballgroßen Süßigkeiten probieren. Lecker! Der perfekte Sonntagsausflug nach Klein-Bangkok. Every weekend the Berlin Thai community meets up at Preußenpark in Wilmersdorf, better known as the Thai Park. On endless rows of blankets they set up portable mini kitchens where the folks prepare, serve, and sell fresh, authentic, and spicy Thai food. For the fainthearted: make sure to tell them to make it mild. Don't forget to get the tasty Thai iced tea and the tennis ball sized sweets. Deeeelicious! A perfect Sunday picnic in Little Bangkok.

Text: Sven Hausherr / Photos: Marta Greber

Preußenpark
Brandenburgische Straße 57, 10713 Berlin-Wilmersdorf
Sat&Sun (weather permitting)

Was man sonst noch in der Gegend rund um den Preußenpark machen kann? Das fragen wir uns auch – Vorschläge an: berlin@ceecee.cc What else is there to do around Preußenpark? Let us know: berlin@ceecee.cc

FRANZÖSISCHE LECKEREIEN & JAPANISCHE SCHREIBWAREN
FRENCH PASTRIES & JAPANESE STATIONERY

Eri ist Japanerin, Toses Wurzeln sind japanisch-französisch. Gemeinsam betreiben sie das Café two and two. Gemeinsam kredenzen sie ihren Gästen hausgemachte Leckereien ihrer Heimatländer. Die Cannelés sind formvollendet, die delikaten Madeleines vorzüglich – ich möchte sofort Marcel Prousts „Auf der Suche nach der verlorenen Zeit“ aufschlagen und verweilen. Eine kleine Auswahl an japanischen Schreibwaren mit Leuchtmarkern, Stiftbeuteln oder portemonnaiegroßen Notizblöckchen ergänzt das Konzept. Diese hier zu verkaufen macht Sinn, da Berliner Cafés doch gerne als Zweitbüro genutzt werden. Der ideale Ort also um Proust nachzueifern oder zumindest Ideen zu notieren und dabei das süße Verlangen zu stillen. Eri hails from Japan and Tose is of mixed French and Japanese descent. The two girls have teamed up to open a French bakery café in Berlin. You'll find a wide variety of delicious sweets, like tarts and patisseries, all made with love. The cannelés are superb and the madeleines here are the best I've ever had; makes me want to read Marcel Proust again. But there is more to this petit café: they also offer Japanese stationery goods such as pens, notebooks, and cases made with traditional machines. In a city where people like using cafés as their second office, selling these items next to cakes and coffee is not such a bad idea. Let's get this novel started or at least take some notes while satisfying a sweet tooth.

Text: Nina Trippel / Photos: Marta Greber

two and two
Pannierstraße 6, 12047 Berlin-Neukölln
Mon-Fri 8:30-18:00, Sat&Sun 10:00-18:00
twoandtwoberlin.com

Immer voll aus gutem Grund: Berlinburger International – der wahrscheinlich kleinste Burgerladen der Stadt ist gleich nebenan, in der Pannierstraße 5. Always busy and for a good reason: Berlinburger International – this is probably the city's smallest burger shop and it's right next door at Pannierstraße 5.

CEE CEE'S GUEST: ARIEL SCHLESINGER

In Ariel Schlesingers Neuköllner Hinterhofatelier stapeln sich Teile alter Türen, Kisten, Metalldrähte und Bohrmaschinen. In zahllosen Kartons findet man mit Sicherheit alle nur erdenklichen Klebstoffe, denn das Kombinieren von zwei oder mehr Gegenständen ist eines seiner künstlerischen Motive, z.B. wenn er eine Papierschere und eine Korrekturbrille absurd miteinander verbindet. Ein bisschen abwegig wirkt auch das kleine Trampolin in seinem Studio. Das findet nicht als Kunstobjekt Verwendung, sondern zum Workout, wie er sagt, und demonstriert es gerne. Überhaupt ist er ein agiler Zeitgenosse – schnellt etwa vom Sofa auf, um seinen Kaktus zu gießen. Davon abgesehen liegt ihm Wasser fern. Er kommt schließlich aus der Wüste, sagt er. Aus Jerusalem, um genau zu sein, wo er geboren wurde und Kunst studierte. Nach einem zweitägigen Aufenthalt 1999 in Berlin wusste er, dass er seine Stadt gefunden hatte. Sieben Jahre später kam er dann wirklich. Erst wollte er keinesfalls nach Neukölln – der Stadtteil schien ihm Tel Aviv zu ähnlich. Heute will er nur noch hier leben: im Lauten und Chaotischen. Und weil er das so mag, treibt es ihn auch gerne mal nach Kreuzberg, und zwar an die Kottbusser Brücke.

Ariel Schlesinger's Neukölln backyard atelier is stacked with old doors, metal wires, drill machines, as well as every type of glue imaginable. He has a passion for creating artwork that involves connecting two or more objects. For example, Ariel combines a pair of paper scissors with some corrective spectacles in a completely absurd way. The trampoline in his studio also looks a bit out of place. It isn't meant for his work but for workouts, and he doesn't mind demonstrating it in front of his visitors. In general, Ariel is an agile fellow, jumping up from the sofa just to water his cactus. Otherwise, he says he's not too interested in water: "I come from the desert." He was born in Jerusalem where he also studied art. After a two-day stay in Berlin in 1999, he knew he had found his city. Seven years later he came to stay. In the beginning he didn't want to live in Neukölln – too much like Tel Aviv, he thought. Today, it's the only place for him: "I feel safer here, in this noisy and chaotic neighborhood." And as he likes this kind of vibe, it also sometimes takes him to the Kottbusser Bridge in Kreuzberg. →

dvirgallery.com
gregorpodnar.com

ABS
1690,-€

Zu verkaufen
Gesamtpreis:
EUR

Zu verkaufen

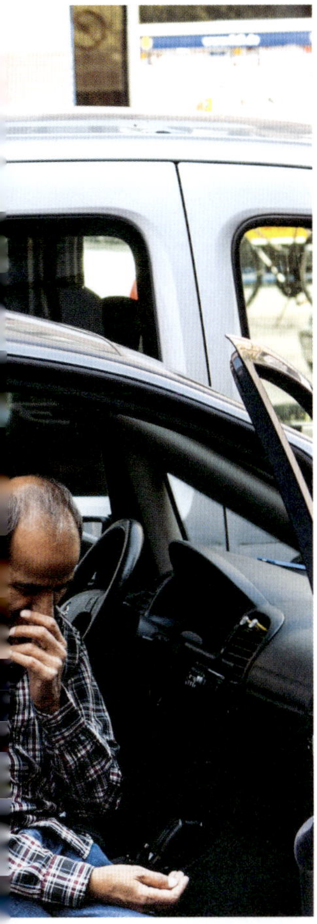

ARIEL SCHLESINGER EMPFIEHLT: AUTOMARKT AUF DER KOTTBUSSER BRÜCKE ARIEL SCHLESINGER RECOMMENDS: KOTTBUSSER BRIDGE CAR MARKET

Der Kottbusser Damm beginnt und endet mit zwei nicht besonders attraktiven Plätzen. Trotzdem haben sowohl Kottbusser Tor als auch Hermannplatz für viele Einwohner ihren Charme – und das zurecht. Was mich auf meinen Stadterkundungen – erst als Tourist und dann als Bewohner – immer angezogen hat, ist die Nutzung des nördlichen Teils des Kottbusser Damms, der bei der Brücke über dem Kanal beginnt und bis zum Kottbusser Tor reicht. Die Straße wird hier als 24-Stunden-Open-Air-Autoflohmarkt genutzt. Wer das Stück entlanggeht, merkt, dass die meisten Autos (und manchmal sogar Boote!), die dort geparkt sind, zum Verkauf stehen. Sie sind blank geputzt und in ihren Fenstern hängen handgeschriebene Zettel, denen man Informationen über die Flitzer entnehmen kann. Mich inspiriert das nicht nur, weil ich, während ich die Straße entlangehe, davon träume, mit einem davon auf der Autobahn herumzudüsen, sondern auch, weil ich es großartig finde, wie dort seit wer weiß wie vielen Jahren ein irgendwie seltsames Verständnis der Nutzung von öffentlichem Raum sichtbar wird. Kottbusser Damm starts and ends with two visually not-so-attractive squares in Berlin. However, both Kottbusser Tor and Hermannplatz still have their charm for many Berliners for different reasons, and rightfully so. What drew me most on my expedition as I explored the city, both as a tourist and later as a resident, was the use of the street between the northern part of Kottbusser Damm, starting at the bridge above the canal, and Kottbusser Tor: a public open air 24 hour used car market. If you walk along, you will notice that most of the cars (and sometimes boats!) that are parked in this section are for sale: all washed up with paper notes in the windows containing attractive handwritten information about these amazing fetchers. This street became an inspiration for me, not only because I dream of myself driving around in many of these cars on the autobahn; but mainly because I find it fascinating that there is this communal understanding of such an awkward use of public space since who knows when – or how it even started.

Text: Ariel Schlesinger / Photos: Benjamin Lindenkreuz

Kottbusser Brücke
Kottbusser Damm, 10967 Berlin-Kreuzberg

Das beste Hummus der Stadt gibt es im kleinen Frühstückslokal von City Chicken (Sonnenallee 59) in Neukölln, findet Ariel; Eingang auf der Weichselstraße. The best hummus in town is offered at the conjoined breakfast spot of City Chicken (Sonnenallee 59) in Neukölln, says Ariel; entrance on Weichselstraße.

BIER, BBQ & MÄNNERRUNDEN
BEER, BBQ & BROMANCE

Bei Chicago Williams wird das ganze Jahr Good Ol'American BBQ aufgetischt. Die Jungs nehmen ihre geräucherten „Fleisch-Angelegenheiten" sehr ernst und bearbeiten ihre Ribs, Briskets oder das Pulled Pork zur Perfektion. Auch sehr zu empfehlen: Das Pastrami. Es wird 21 Tage in Pökellake und im Anschluss 48 Stunden in Trockenmarinade eingelegt, bevor es schließlich geräuchert und gedämpft wird. Die hausgemachte Hot-Sauce schmeckt unglaublich: Mit ihrer idealen Schärfe verleiht sie den Speisen den Extra-Kick! Dazu gibt's klassische Beilagen wie Macaroni & Cheese, Backed Beans, Mashed Potaotes mit Gravy und inzwischen sogar eigenes Bier. Und das alles in sehr entspannter Atmosphäre und, wen wundert's, mit einem Überschuss an Männern rundherum. Summer may be coming to an end, but that doesn't mean that BBQ season should. Lucky for us, Chicago Williams serves good ol' American BBQ all year round. Mind you, the style has nothing to do with Chicago, but rather a creation of their own. The guys here take their smoked meats seriously and work their pulled pork, brisket, ribs, and chicken to perfection. Don't skip out on the pastrami: it's brine-cured for 21 days and dry-rubbed for 48 hours before finally getting smoked and steamed. Their new homemade hot sauce is outstanding with just the right amount of spiciness to add a kick to your meal. Plus they've got basic sides like mac and cheese and baked beans, a solid selection of German microbrewed beers, and a laid-back, friendly atmosphere. The joint is packed every night with a noticeably high man-to-woman ratio – now you know why!

Text: Rei Matsuoka / Photos: Marta Greber

Chicago Williams BBQ
Hannoversche Straße 2, 10115 Berlin-Mitte
Daily 17:00-24:00
chicagowilliamsbbq.de

Wenn es im Chicago Williams BBQ zu voll sein sollte: eine gute Alternative für Pastrami und andere Fleischgerichte ist Ruben & Carla in der Linienstraße 136.
If Chicago Williams BBQ is packed, check out Ruben & Carla at Linienstraße 136 – a good alternative for pastrami and other meats.

Keine Zeit nach Lichtenberg zu fahren? Miss Saigon in der Skalitzer Straße 38 in Kreuzberg befriedigt immerhin kulinarische Gelüste mit südvietnamesischer Küche. No time to head to Lichtenberg? Try Miss Saigon at Skalitzer Straße 38 in Kreuzberg for some southern Vietnamese cuisine.

SHOPPING AUF VIETNAMESISCH
VIETNAMESE STYLE SHOPPING

Falls Du einen neuen Haarschnitt nötig hast oder shoppen musst, und das am Sonntag, falls Du hungrig bist oder einfach etwas Besonderes erleben willst – dann steig in die Tram M8 und an der Endhaltestelle erwartet dich eine urban-abenteuerliche Welt – das Dong Xuan Center. Angesiedelt auf einem Industriegelände, schaut man hier leider nicht auf die romantische Halong-Bucht, aber dafür betritt man einen typisch vietnamesischen Markt mit all seinen Gerüchen, Geräuschen und Menschen. In den vier geräumigen und vollgestopften Hallen kann man sich wahlweise eine Maniküre machen lassen – Schwäne vor Schneelandschaft etwa –, einen Katzenaschenbecher kaufen, einen Ausflug ins Kunstblumenuniversum wagen, pinke Früchte oder neonfarbenes Gelee in den Einkaufskorb legen, Snacks mit unaussprechlichem Namen verzehren oder ganz einfach: eine authentische Phở genießen oder Bun Thit Nuong, auf Kohle gegrilltes Schweinefleisch mit Reisnudeln und frischen Kräutern – eine Spezialität aus Hanoi. Mein favorisierter Lebensmittelhändler befindet sich in Halle 3, gleich beim Eingang, und mein liebster Essensstand direkt gegenüber. It's Sunday and you need a haircut, amazing food, and some retail therapy. Then take the M8 and your journey will lead you to an exotic, urban reality. At the Dong Xuan Center, located in what was once a decrepit industrial field, you won't be gazing romantically at the Ha Long Bay; instead, you'll be amid the hustle and bustle of a Vietnamese market – with its people, sound, and scent. In the four spacious halls, you can get your nails done in contemporary baroque style with tigers and swans against a snowy landscape, buy a small cat ashtray, enjoy a plastic dream in the fake flower heaven, or get pink fruit, neon mint jello, and snacks with unpronounceable names and indescribable textures. Or simply enjoy an authentic Phở soup; I thought my mom was the only person who made it so good. Try a Bun Thit Nuong – charcoal grilled pork with rice noodles and fresh herbs, a typical dish from beautiful Hanoi. My favorite grocery store is located in Hall 3 to the right of the entrance and my favorite restaurant is to the left.

Text: Tutia Schaad / Photos: Sasha Kharchenko

Dong Xuan Center
Herzbergstraße 128-139, 10365 Berlin-Lichtenberg
Wed-Mon 11:00-20:00

Von Instanbul nach New York in zwei Sekunden: auf ein Stück Kuchen zu Princess Cheesecake in die Tucholskystraße 37. From Istanbul to New York in two seconds: for a real treat, enjoy a slice of Princess Cheesecake at Tucholskystraße 37.

ERLESENE TÜRKISCHE SÜSSIGKEITEN TRADITIONAL TURKISH DELIGHTS

Berlin hat die größte türkische Community außerhalb der Türkei – trotzdem ist es gar nicht so leicht, hier authentische türkische Süßigkeiten zu finden. Bei Confiserie Orientale, der einzigen Filiale des 1883 in Istanbul gegründeten Traditionsbetriebs außerhalb der Türkei, findet man sie: feinstes Lokum und Marzipan sowie Mokka, extra stark. Ich komme gerne hierher, um etwas Süßes im Café zu essen, aber die Leckereien sind auch ein ideales Mitbringsel, wenn man bei Freunden eingeladen ist.
Although Berlin has the largest Turkish community outside of Turkey, it is not easy to find authentic Turkish delicacies here. At the Confiserie Orientale you will find the most delicious Turkish delights (lokum), as well as marzipan and strong mocha coffees to level out the sweet taste in your mouth. Founded in 1883 in Istanbul, it is still run by the same family. The shop on Linienstraße is the only one outside of Turkey. I like enjoying the sweets at the café but they also make a perfect gift to bring along when visiting friends.

Text: Sven Hausherr / Photos: Ailine Liefeld

Confiserie Orientale
Linienstraße 113, 10115 Berlin-Mitte
Tue-Fri 11:00-19:00, Sat&Sun 11:00-18:00
confiserie-orientale-berlin.com

CLASSICS

ERÖFFNUNG WIRD IN BERLIN JEDEN TAG GEFEIERT. ZEITGLEICH VERSCHWINDET LEISE ETWAS. ANDERES ÜBERDAUERT DIE ZEIT, DEN WANDEL, DIE GESCHMÄCKER. HIERHER KEHREN WIR IMMER WIEDER ZURÜCK. A NEW PLACE POPS UP WHILE ANOTHER ONE BITES THE DUST ON A DAILY BASIS IN BERLIN. CHANGES ARE GOOD, BUT ONLY SOME WILL STAND THE TEST OF TIME.

EIN KUNST-SPAZIERGANG DURCHS 20. JAHRHUNDERT
A WALK THROUGH 20TH CENTURY ART

Im Museum Berggruen wartet kein klassisches Arrangement auf den Besucher – im Gegenteil: Die Räume sind warm und intim, die Gemälde individuell gerahmt, Bänke laden zum Verweilen ein. Beim Durchschreiten der Ausstellungsräume zieht das 20. Jahrhundert an einem vorbei: das ausschweifende Leben der 1920er-Jahre, die Krisen und die Kriege. Gleichzeitig nimmt man an persönlichen Momenten der Künstler teil. So werden Picasso, Klee oder Giacometti zu Freunden, Liebhabern oder Weggefährten – eine unvergessliche Zeitreise. Auch afrikanische Kunst, die oftmals Inspirationsquelle der gezeigten Meister war, findet hier ihren Platz. Die Gegenüberstellung zeigt spannende Zusammenhänge und Parallelen. Und auch der schöne Garten mit Skulpturenensemble ist für die Besucher geöffnet. No institutional atmosphere awaits the visitors at the Berggruen Museum. Quite the opposite, actually: the rooms are warm and intimate. The paintings are individually framed and benches invite you to linger. Walking through the exhibition halls is like watching the 20th century pass by – the excessive life of the Roaring 20s, crises, and wars – while allowing viewers to participate in the artists' personal moments. Picasso, Klee, and Giacometti become your companions, friends, or lovers – an unforgettable journey through time. Besides that, African art, which was often a source of inspiration for the masters shown, is housed here offering fascinating connections and parallels. The beautiful sculpture garden is also open to visitors.

Text: Olga Schlosser / Photos: HC Krass, Karolina Rosina

Museum Berggruen
Schloßstraße 1, 14059 Berlin-Charlottenburg
Tue-Fri 10:00-18:00, Sat & Sun 11:00-18:00
smb.museum/museen-und-einrichtungen/museum-berggruen/home

Nach der Tour im Museum: eine Runde in den Schlosspark Charlottenburg. Besonders schön ist es am Belvedere-Pavillon mit Blick auf den Karpfenteich. Upon leaving the museum, take a breath of fresh air by walking through the park. Belvedere Pavilion offers a picturesque view of the pond and Charlottenburg Palace.

C L A S S I C S

DAS ZUHAUSE DER DESIGN-KLASSIKER DESIGN CLASSICS REVISITED

Das Bauhaus-Archiv bei einem Spaziergang zufällig zu entdecken – eher unwahrscheinlich. Zu übersehen ist das von Walter Gropius erbaute Gebäude direkt am Landwehrkanal zwischen Botschaften und CDU-Parteizentrale allerdings nicht. Über die Brücke geht es ins Innere des Gebäudes. Hier wird die Klassische Moderne von Skizzen bis zu Objekten präsentiert. Wer mehr Zeit hat: Im hellen Innenhof lohnt am Wochenende ein Brunch oder Frühstück im hauseigenen Café mit anschließender Führung. It's pretty unlikely to stumble across the Bauhaus Archive while you're out on a walk. The museum built by Walter Gropius is located on the Landwehr Canal, between embassies and the headquarters of the Christian Democratic Party – not the most popular destinations per se. Once you're there, however, you can't miss it. Follow the bridge to the heart of the architectural complex. The collection features original examples of classic modernism – from sketches to objects designed by the members of the world-famous design school. Breakfast or brunch in the bright courtyard café followed by a guided tour is the best way to begin your Bauhaus expedition.

Text: Max von Thadden / Photos: Karsten Hintz, Hartwig Klappert, Gunter Lepkowski

Bauhaus-Archiv
Klingelhöferstraße 14, 10785 Berlin-Tiergarten
Wed–Mon 10:00–17:00
bauhaus.de

Wer tiefer in die Bauhaus-Geschichte eintauchen will, besucht das Mies van der Rohe Haus in Hohenschönhausen in der Oberseestraße 60, das aktuell für Ausstellungen genutzt wird. If you want to see more Bauhaus art and architecture, visit the Mies van der Rohe Haus at Oberseestraße 60 in Hohenschönhausen. It currently serves as an exhibition space.

CEE CEE'S GUEST: TIM SEIFERT

Wenn man bei Tim zum Geburtstag eingeladen ist, sind zwei Dinge garantiert: Es wird ein gutes Stück Fleisch gegrillt und es geht gen Grunewald. Timmi, wie ihn alle nennen, ist bekennender Foodie und schätzt die gastronomische Vielfalt der Stadt. Und die Gegend, in der er aufgewachsen ist. Vor allem die Wälder und Seen Zehlendorfs, Dahlems und rund um den Wannsee – Teile Berlins „die viele Menschen in meinem aktuellen Kiez gar nicht kennen oder wertschätzen", wie er sagt. Er pendelt aber nicht nur zwischen Mitte und dem Westen – er ist weltweit unterwegs. Das ist Teil seiner Geschäftsstrategie: 2009 hat er zusammen mit Frederik Frede und Torsten Bergler das Interview-Magazin Freunde von Freunden gegründet. Die Porträtierten sind in aller Welt zu Hause – und zeigen es, ihr Zuhause. Inzwischen ist FvF zur Produktionsagentur mit internationalen Kunden herangewachsen und bringt viel Arbeit mit sich. In seiner Freizeit trifft man Timmi mit Sicherheit in herausragenden Spezialitätengeschäften, denn „wer Berlin kennt, kann hier fast alles haben". Guten Käse auf jeden Fall. Wo? Bei Maître Philippe & Filles. If you are invited to Tim's birthday party, expect to find these two things: great tasting grilled meat and a way to Grunewald. Timmi, as everyone calls him, is a foodie who appreciates the culinary diversity of Berlin and the neighborhood he grew up in. Apart from that, he loves the woods and lakes in Zehlendorf, Dahlem, and Wannsee – parts of Berlin which, according to Tim, are underappreciated by most locals. He not only commutes between his apartment in Mitte and the city's West, but also travels the world: it's a part of his business strategy. In 2009, he and his partners, Frederik Frede and Torsten Bergler, founded the interview magazine Freunde von Freunden. It features people from all over the world in their homes and shares insights into exactly this, their homes. Meanwhile, FvF has grown into a production agency with international clients. This means a lot of work – but during his spare time you'll likely run into him in excellent gourmet shops. "If you know Berlin well, you can find almost anything here," he says. There's certainly fantastic cheese. Where? At Maître Philippe & Filles. →

freundevonfreunden.com

Welche Institution im Westen wird ihrem Ruf gerecht? Die Paris Bar in der Kantstraße 152, sagt Timmi. Which institution in the West lives up to its reputation? Paris Bar at Kantstraße 152, says Timmi.

TIM SEIFERT EMPFIEHLT: MAÎTRE PHILIPPE & FILLES

TIM SEIFERT RECOMMENDS: MAÎTRE PHILIPPE & FILLES

Getreu dem Motto „Give me a good sharp knife and a good sharp cheese and I'm a happy man" (George R. R. Martin) ist das Geschäft Maître Philippe & Filles ein Traum für jeden Feinschmecker und Liebhaber guten Käses. Als Charlottenburger Junge absolvierte ich mein erstes Schulpraktikum bei „California Boarding" in der Emser Straße; den Laden gibt es dort leider nicht mehr, aber bei vielen Berliner Skatern gilt er immer noch als eine Art Institution. Auf meinem Hin- und Rückweg zum Bus Richtung Shop lief ich damals fast täglich an einem kleinen französischen Laden vorbei: Maître Philippe. Erst knapp zehn Jahre später kam ich das erste Mal in den Genuss der angebotenen Käse, Weine und Öle. Das Personal stellt für jeden Geschmack das passende Käsemenü zusammen. Ich selbst sehe mich weniger als Experte, esse aber wahnsinnig gerne und bin neugierig – daher weiß ich die Beratung sehr zu schätzen. Wer noch mehr Service möchte, stellt am besten ein paar Fragen zu Herkunft und Herstellung, denn die Geschichten machen Hunger – ähnlich wie eine Live-Kochsendung, nur nicht so plump und dafür mit exzellentem Fachwissen gespickt. If you can attest to the quote "Give me a good sharp knife and a good sharp cheese and I'm a happy man." (George R. R. Martin), then Maître Philippe is an excellent place for you to visit. I used to pass by this little store practically everyday when I was a Charlottenburg-based kid, interning at a skate shop called "California Boarding" on Emser Straße; unfortunately the shop doesn't exist anymore, but loads of skaters will remember it as an institution. It took me almost ten years to step inside to enjoy the fine French foods offered there: cheese, wine, and oil. The shop staff will happily create your personal cheese selection according to your taste. I don't consider myself to be a connoisseur, but a curious eater who appreciates the advice. You should ask a few questions about their products, like the origin and manufacturing process – the stories are remarkable and will make you hungry – just like watching a cooking show but less "cheesy" and full of expert knowledge.

Text: Tim Seifert / Photos: Benjamin Lindenkreuz

Maître Philippe & Filles
Emser Straße 42, 10719 Berlin-Charlottenburg
Tue-Fri 10:00-19:00, Sat 10:00-14:00
maitrephilippe.de

EINES WIE KEINES: DAS KINO INTERNATIONAL A CINEMA LIKE NO OTHER: KINO INTERNATIONAL

Wer das Kino International aufsucht, wird daran erinnert, worum es eigentlich geht: den Film. Hier, im ehemaligen DDR-Premierenkino und Prestigeobjekt der sozialistischen Architektur der Moderne, setzt man auf Reduktion. Das Gebäude aus dem Jahr 1963 ist schlicht, das Filmprogramm ausgewählt, und es gibt nur einen einzigen Kinosaal. Der Weg dorthin führt durch das eindrucksvolle Foyer im Obergeschoss, das Herzstück des Kinos. Mit seinen Sitzinseln lädt es dazu ein, vor oder nach dem Film zu verweilen. Der Blick durch die Panoramafenster direkt auf den Fernsehturm erinnert trotz aller Ruhe daran, dass man sich mitten in Berlin befindet. At Kino International, visitors are reminded of what cinema is all about: the film. The former GDR theater is simple and unadorned, but the large building scores high for its pleasant design, clear structure, and the carefully curated film selection. The movies are shown in a large auditorium; pass through the impressive foyer on the first floor to get there. The comfy seats will make you want to stay and have a drink – before or after the film. The foyer's windows offer a panoramic view of the TV Tower, which gently reminds you of the fact that you're sitting in an oasis of tranquility in the center of Berlin.

Nach dem Film: Statt ein Taxi nach Hause zu nehmen, lieber laufen – diese Straße, dieser Blick! After the film: what's better than taking a cab home? Walking down Karl-Marx-Allee, a one of a kind street!

Text: Cedric Retzmann / Photos: Daniel Horn, Yorck Kinogruppe

Kino International
Karl-Marx-Allee 33, 10178 Berlin-Mitte
kino-international.com

EIN AUSFLUG IN DEN BRITZER GARTEN A TRIP TO BEAUTIFUL BRITZER GARDEN

Jedes Jahr im Frühling blühen im Britzer Garten die Rhododendren – und werden gerne als „Zauberblüten" angepriesen. Das ist vielleicht ein wenig übertrieben, aber hübsch anzusehen ist das kleine Areal in voller Blüte auf jeden Fall. Auch rundherum und das ganze Jahr ist der Garten eine wunderbare Stadtoase. Der kleine Teich wird nicht nur von Enten bevölkert, sondern auch von ferngesteuerten Booten und bietet daher neben aller Idylle auch viel Entertainment. Das Wichtigste: Proviant fürs Picknick nicht vergessen! Britzer Garden calls them "Zauberblüten" (magic flowers): perhaps a slight exaggeration, but the beautiful rhododendrons in full bloom in spring are indeed something to wonder and marvel at. The area next to the little grove is one of the nicest spots in the park. As for entertainment: don't forget to check out the remote controlled boats on the lake and bring your own picnic. With a magnificent natural setting like this, it's the thing to do.

Text: Nina Trippel / Photos: Benjamin Lindenkreuz

Britzer Garten
Buckower Damm 146, 12349 Berlin-Britz
Daily 9:00 until dark
gruen-berlin.de

Wer ein Neuköllner Souvenir mit in seinen Kiez bringen will: In der Britzer Mühle am Buckower Damm 130 kann man frisch gemahlenes Mehl erwerben.
If you're looking for a Neukölln souvenir to bring home, you can buy fresh milled flour at Britz Mill at Buckower Damm 130.

CEE CEE'S GUEST: ETTINA BERRIOS-NEGRÓN

Berlin nimmt es nicht so streng mit dem Herkunftsnachweis: Berliner nennen darf sich, wer in jungen Jahren hierhergezogen ist und die Stadt durch Kinderaugen gesehen hat. So wie Ettina Berrios-Negrón. Im Westen aufgewachsen, hat sie die Charlottenburger und Wilmersdorfer Welt von klein auf beäugt und später in Schöneberg im Lette-Verein Mode studiert. An vielen Orten im Westen der Stadt hängt auch heute noch ihr Herz – zum Beispiel an eingesessenen Betrieben und Spezialgeschäften wie dem Kulturbuchladen Bücherbogen. Wohnhaft ist Ettina heute in Mitte, im Ex-Osten, denn ihr eigenes Geschäft passt hierher am besten: die Boutique Thone Negrón. Boutique? Genau. Wo andere Geschäfte sich Shop nennen und auf kühle Schlichtheit setzen, hat die Designerin ein liebevoll gestaltetes Kleinod geschaffen, in dem sich die Dame von Welt einkleiden kann (s. S. 158). In Mode, die im Ganzen sehr erwachsen ist, im Detail jedoch verspielt: Kleine Glasknöpfe, die eigentlich für Puppen gedacht sind, schmücken beispielsweise Ettinas Entwürfe. Ein bisschen sieht sie die Welt eben immer noch durch Kinderaugen. Wo sie ihre Inspiration findet? Im Westen natürlich, im Georg Kolbe Museum. Berlin is not strict about who it calls its own: someone who moved to Berlin at a young age and has explored the city ever since would definitely qualify as a Berliner. This holds true for Ettina Berrios-Negrón. Raised in West Berlin, she grew up admiring the worlds of Charlottenburg and Wilmersdorf, and later continued her love affair with the West by studying fashion at the Lette-Verein in Schöneberg. Today, she is still attached to some of the long-established stores of West Berlin, such as the culture bookstore Bücherbogen. Nevertheless, she packed her bags and moved to Mitte, the former East, because this is where her own store fits in best: the Thone Negrón Boutique (s. p. 158). The designer has created a beautiful shop for fashion consumption. The style is all in all very grown up but with playful details: small glass buttons originally intended for doll clothes adorn her designs. In her own way, she still sees the world through a child's eyes. Where does she find inspiration? At the Georg Kolbe Museum for example – which is in the West, of course. →

thonenegron.com

ETTINA BERRIOS-NEGRÓN EMPFIEHLT: GEORG KOLBE MUSEUM UND CAFÉ K

ETTINA BERRIOS-NEGRÓN RECOMMENDS: GEORG KOLBE MUSEUM AND CAFÉ K

Mitten im tiefsten Charlottenburg steht das Atelierhaus-Ensemble des Bildhauers Georg Kolbe. In den 1920er-Jahren ließ er es als Wohn- und Arbeitsplatz für sich und seine Familie erbauen; heutzutage öffnet es als Museum mit wechselnden Ausstellungen seine Türen. Im ehemaligen Maleratelier ist das Café K eingezogen, dessen Interieur mit seinen zurückhaltenden Farbtönen beinahe unberührt wirkt. Von hier aus blickt man auf den schlicht gehaltenen Skulpturengarten mit Kiefern und Bronzefiguren des Künstlers. Um sich für einen Ausflug zum Teufelsberg zu stärken, empfiehlt sich ein Sonnenplatz auf der Terrasse. Die teilt man unter der Woche mit reizenden älteren Damen und Herren – vor allem jedoch mit Damen –, die zum Kaffeetrinken oder Mittagessen vorbeikommen. Das Georg Kolbe Museum ist der perfekte Ort, um ein fast vergessenes Stück Berlin kennenzulernen und sich in das alte Charlottenburg einzufühlen.

The studio complex of sculptor Georg Kolbe is located in the heart of Charlottenburg and was built as a residence and workspace for himself and his family in the 1920s. Today, it is a museum with rotating exhibitions. The former painting studio was converted to the Café K; with its simple interior, the space almost looks untouched by time. From the café, you have a view of the simple sculpture garden with pine trees and bronze figures by the artist. In order to energize yourself for the trek up Teufelsberg ("Devil's Mountain") later, take a seat on the sunny terrace - you will most likely share a table with lovely elder ladies. This museum is the perfect place to learn about an almost-forgotten piece of Berlin history and to discover Charlottenburg.

Text: Ettina Berrios-Negrón / Photos: Serge Hasenböhler, Karolina Rosina

Georg Kolbe Museum & Café K
Sensburger Allee 25-26, 14055 Berlin-Westend
Tue-Sun 10:00-18:00
georg-kolbe-museum.de

Schnelles Mittagessen in Mitte? Ettina empfiehlt: auf eine Ofenkartoffel oder einen Salat zu Joris in der Brunnenstraße 158. A quick lunch in Mitte? Ettina's recommendation: Enjoy a baked potato or salad at Joris at Brunnenstraße 158.

DER GOURMET-FISCHHANDEL MIT SCHLEMMERECKE A GOURMET FISH MARKET & RESTAURANT

Eher durch Zufall bin ich auf das Rogacki, die angeblich beste Adresse für Feinkost im alten Westen, gestoßen. Zwischen all den Geschäften übersieht man den Laden auch leicht, der von außen so gar nichts Feines an sich hat. Aber lass Dich nicht von der Fassade und dem 1970er-Interieur irritieren: Hier gibt's den real Deal – lebenden Fisch in großer Auswahl, Fleisch und allerlei andere Spezialitäten. Und das schon seit 1928. Das Beste ist aber eigentlich das "Schlemmereck" – Treffpunkt für Alt-Berliner Gourmets. Wenn man sich auf die spezielle Atmosphäre einlässt, bekommt man hier hervorragende Tagesgerichte frisch zubereitet: Scampi auf Saisongemüse oder Surf'n'Turf. Gerne führe ich meinen Berlin-Besuch am Samstagmittag her, obwohl es schon mal schwierig werden kann, einen der begehrten Plätze an den Stehtischen oder der Theke zu bekommen. Aber auch wenn es hektisch ist, bleibt die Stimmung immer locker. Sollte es mal wieder etwas länger dauern, freuen sich die Gäste bisweilen über ein Gläschen Federweißer. Ich bin dem verblassten Westberliner Charme des Rogacki gänzlich erlegen.

It was only by chance that I came across Rogacki, presumably the best address for fine food in the former West Berlin. Between all the stores along the street, it's easy to miss this shop that doesn't seem to offer anything "fine" at all from the outside. But don't be deceived by the façade and the outdated interior design because you'll find real delicacies here: fresh and live fish, the best meats and cold cuts, and loads of other specialties – since 1928. The best part is the "Schlemmereck," a meeting place for Berlin's well-established gourmets. If you are open to the unique atmosphere, you can enjoy excellent specials that are prepared freshly. It might be scampi with seasonal vegetables or a top-notch surf'n'turf. Every now and then I go there with my Berlin-Mitte visitors on a Saturday afternoon, though it's sometimes hard to find a place at one of the bar tables. Even when busy, the place keeps its laid-back vibe and guests enjoy a glass of Federweisser on the house, if they have a longer wait. I, for one, totally fell for Rogacki's faded old West Berlin charm!

Text: Oliver Moore / Photos: Marta Greber

Rogacki
Wilmersdorfer Straße 145/146, 10585 Berlin-Charlottenburg
Mon-Wed 9:00-18:00, Thu 9:00-19:00, Fri 8:00-19:00, Sat 8:00-16:00
rogacki.de

Auch delikat: eine Leberkässemmel bei Feines aus Österreich in der Leonhardtstraße 11 in Charlottenburg.
Also yummy: a "Leberkässemmel" (a sandwich with cold cuts) at Feines aus Österreich at Leonhardtstraße 11 in Charlottenburg.

SAVIGNY PASSAGE
DiENE
DiENER

DAS TRADITIONSLOKAL FÜR DEUTSCHE HAUSMANNSKOST

THE TRADITIONAL RESTAURANT FOR GERMAN FARE

Um die Jahrhundertwende war das Backsteingebäude in der Grolmanstraße Casino und Restaurant für den "Tattersall des Westens", wo sich die Damen der Gesellschaft nach dem Ausritt ein Gläschen Champagner zur Erfrischung gönnten. Ab 1954 wurde das Restaurant von Franz Diener – einem ehemaligen Deutschen Meister im Schwergewicht – betrieben und etablierte sich schnell als Treffpunkt der Boheme. Zahlreiche Portraits von Künstlern, die eine Affinität zum Boxsport und vor allem zur berühmten hausgemachten Leberwurst des gelernten Fleischers hatten, findet man noch heute an den Wänden. Besonders köstlich sind die Klassiker der deutschen Küche: Bouletten, Königsberger Klopse und Eier in Senfsauce – auch, weil sie von der wohl charmantesten Kellnerin Berlins serviert werden. Around the turn of the 20th century, this red brick building on Grolmanstraße was a casino and restaurant, where society ladies would treat themselves to a glass of champagne after going for a ride at the nearby "Tattersall" (horse-riding hall). In 1954, the restaurant was taken over by Franz Diener, a former German heavyweight champion, and quickly established itself as an artists' bar. Today the walls are still covered with numerous portraits by artists with a penchant for boxing and Diener's famous homemade liver pâté. You will find traditional and classic German dishes like rissoles, potato salad, Königsberger Klopse (German meatballs), and eggs in mustard sauce. The food here is delicious, particularly because it is served by the most charming waitress in Berlin.

Text: Antje Drinkuth / Photos: Marta Greber

Diener Tattersall
Grolmanstraße 47, 10623 Berlin-Charlottenburg
Daily from 18:00

Auch ein Haus mit Tradition: C. Adolph am Savignyplatz 3 – das Sammelsurium für Haushaltshelfer und Spezialbedarf. Another West Berlin institution: C. Adolph at Savignyplatz 3 – the store that has everything for your home.

OBERBAUMBRÜCKE, KREUZBERG

STIMMT
GEGEN KRIEG
WÄHLT PSG
PSG

PLANET
ESTER
MERLIN
MIKE

WEINBERGSPARK, MITTE

ROSENTHALER PLATZ, MITTE

THE
easyHotel.com
Simple comfort, great value.
U
Rosenthaler Platz
CHINA FOOD
porta
DER MÖBELGIGANT
IN POTSDAM
BAHAMA
LEISURE
JEFFREY LEWIS
& THE JRAMS
ON TOUR

LEIPZIGER STRASSE, MITTE

Coca-Cola

SHO RT LI ST

ÜBERALL DORT, WO ZEITGEIST ZU HAUSE IST, ERFINDEN SICH STADT UND BEWOHNER NEU – SECHS TRENDS, DIE UNS BEGLEITEN: DRINNEN, DRAUSSEN UND UNTERWEGS.

WHEN ZEITGEIST MOVES IN, THE CITY AND ITS RESIDENTS CHANGE THEIR WAYS – SIX TRENDS THAT ACCOMPANY US: INDOORS, OUTDOORS, AND ON THE GO.

Chapter One
Mittenwalder Straße 30
10961 Berlin-Kreuzberg
chapter-one-coffee.com

Oslo Kaffebar
Eichendorffstraße 13
10115 Berlin-Mitte
oslokaffebar.com

Andraschko Kaffeemanufaktur
Industriestraße 18
12099 Berlin-Tempelhof
(Shop only)
andraschkokaffee.com

COFFEE CITY

Bonanza Coffee
Oderberger Straße 35
10435 Berlin-Prenzlauer Berg
bonanzacoffee.de

Café 9
Eisenbahnstraße 42
10997 Berlin-Kreuzberg
markthalleneun.de

Dank der „Third Wave" ist Berlin in Kaffeefragen ganz weit vorne und zeigt uns, dass der Weg der Bohne vom Strauch bis in die Tasse keine Nebensache ist. Im Gegensatz zur Coffee Art – die ist nur die Oberflächenkrönung auf dem Flat White. Die wahre Kunst aber liegt darin, zu wissen: welche Bohnen, welche Röstung, welche Maschine. Und: Cold Brew, Pour Over oder Drip Coffee? Zum Mitnehmen? Nein, zum Genießen vor Ort!

Berliners know the journey of the bean from the coffee nursery to the cup is no small matter, thanks to the "Third Wave of Coffee." Latte art is pleasing to the eyes and the taste buds, but the real key to enjoying coffee is to know the origin and quality of the bean, roast types, and the roasting machine used. Cold brew, pour over, or drip? To go? No no, for here!

Blaue Bohnen
Seumestraße 14
10245 Berlin-Friedrichshain
(Shop only)
blauebohnen.com

The Barn Roastery
Schönhauser Allee 8
10119 Berlin-Prenzlauer Berg
barn.bigcartel.com

Five Elephant
Reichenberger Straße 101
10999 Berlin-Kreuzberg
fiveelephant.com

Daniel's Eatery
danielseatery.com

Rosebud
facebook.com/rosebudsupperclubberlin

Mother's Mother
mothersmother.com

SUPER SUPPER CLUBS

Brotzeit at List
Weichselstraße 66
12043 Berlin-Neukölln
daslist.de

Private Dinnerrunden sind weltweit im Trend, aber so facettenreich wie in Berlin wird selten zu Tisch gebeten. Passionierte Köche und Gastgeber, Laien und Profis laden zum Festmahl. Dazu gehören Familienrezepte, die traditionelle Brotzeit, Gourmet-Menüs mit Märchenwelt-Setting oder kulinarische Hommagen an Künstler, Picknicks im Grünen und und und. Neue Freunde gibt's spätestens zum Dessert. Private dinners are a worldwide trend, but rarely do cities offer such a wide range: closely guarded family recipes, countryside picnics, traditional German "Brotzeit," or culinary homages to artists. Whether laymen or professional, there is one thing in common between all cooks and hosts: passion. New friends come with dessert.

I eat you
ieatyou.de

Thyme at Muse
Immanuelkirchstraße 31
Berlin-Prenzlauer Berg
thyme-supperclub.com

Fortuna's Table
Weserstraße 58
12045 Berlin-Neukölln
fortunastable.de

Speisenklub Neukölln
facebook.com/speisenklubneukoelln

Krauted Haus
krauted-haus.com

Prinzessinnengärten
Prinzenstraße 35 - 38
10969 Berlin-Kreuzberg
prinzessinnengarten.net

Infarm
Glogauer Straße 6
10999 Berlin-Kreuzberg
infarm.de

Gemeinschaftsgarten Allmende-Kontor
Tempelhofer Freiheit
Oderstraße 50
12049 Berlin-Neukölln
allmende-kontor.de

Für Urban Gardening-Anhänger ist Berlin eine Spielwiese, denn die Stadt wächst und gedeiht: Das Parkhausdeck wird zur Kleingarten-Alternative und die Brachfläche zum Acker. Mit Gießkanne und Saatgut bewaffnet macht man sich gerne die Hände schmutzig und erntet das Abendessen auf Hochbeeten ab. Oder kauft sich den Indoor-Garten für die Altbauwohnung.

Berlin is growing and thriving in every aspect. Parking garage rooftops are turned into gardens and empty lands are converted into oases. For local urban gardening enthusiasts, the sky is the limit. So dig in: sow, grow, and cook your own harvest. Alternatively set up an indoor garden in your apartment or make good use of your small balcony.

Etagen Erika
etagen-erika.de

URBAN GARDENS

Klunkerkranich
Karl-Marx-Straße 66
12043 Berlin-Neukölln
klunkerkranich.de

Himmelbeet
Ruheplatzstraße 12
13347 Berlin-Wedding
himmelbeet.com

Our/Berlin
ourvodka.com/berlin

ManuTeeFaktur
manuteefaktur.com

Shukran
shukran.de

TAKE A SIP

SHORTLIST

Bier, Eistee, Spirituosen oder Limonade: Immer mehr Getränke werden in Berlin produziert – von Nachwuchsbrauern und Autodidakten. Manchmal mit einer großen Firma im Rücken, oft in Eigenregie. Hier eine Auswahl für die Sommererfrischung, ein wärmendes Wintergetränk, das Feierabendbier oder fürs Catering. Craft beer, iced tea, spirits, and soft drinks from young brewers and self-taught visionaries – some with big companies backing them up, but more often on their own – beverage production is increasing in Berlin. Here is our selection: from summer refreshments to warm winter drinks to after work beer to party booze.

Berliner Sommer / Winter
berlinerwinter.de

Fountain of Youth & Michelberger Booze
michelbergerbooze.com
michelbergermonkey.com

Wildkräuter
wild-kraeuter.com

Los Angeles Cold Press
lacoldpress.com

Talent
talent-tee.de

Good Spirits
goodspirits.co

Borgmann 1772
borgmann1772.com

Quartiermeister
quartiermeister.org

Berliner Bierfabrik
bierfabrik.info

Vagabund
vagabundbrauerei.com

ART MADNESS

Kraupa-Tuskany Zeidler
Karl-Liebknecht-Straße 29
10178 Berlin-Mitte
aktnz.com

Autocenter
Leipziger Straße 56
10117 Berlin-Mitte
autocenterart.de

Johann König at St. Agnes
Alexandrinenstraße 118-121
10969 Berlin-Kreuzberg
johannkoenig.de

Sprüth Magers
Oranienburger Straße 18
10178 Berlin-Mitte
spruethmagers.com

Nach dem Mauerfall waren die Ateliers günstig, die Fabrikhallen leer und Weißwein kaufte man kistenweise auf Vorrat. Manche Künstler und Galeristen blieben nur kurz, andere bis heute. Und es werden jährlich mehr. Genau wie die Kunstveranstaltungen. Das Gallery Weekend lockt im Frühjahr, die Berlin Biennale jeden zweiten Sommer, die Berlin Art Week und die Kunstmesse abc im Herbst, und auch das restliche Jahr über herrscht kein Mangel an Openings – hier eine Auswahl für den donnerstäglichen Eröffnungsmarathon. After the fall of the Berlin Wall, studios were cheap, factory buildings were empty, and white wine was sold by the case. Many young artists and gallerists emerged; some remained. Today the city hosts the Gallery Weekend Berlin in spring, Berlin Biennale every other summer, as well as Berlin Art Week and art fair abc in fall. As for the rest of the year, save Thursday evening for gallery openings around town.

Peres Projects
Karl-Marx-Allee 82
10243 Berlin-Friedrichshain
peresprojects.com

Thomas Fischer
Potsdamer Straße 77-87 House H
10785 Berlin-Tiergarten
galeriethomasfischer.de

VW (VeneKlasen/Werner)
Rudi-Dutschke-Straße 26
10969 Berlin-Kreuzberg
vwberlin.com

PSM
Köpenicker Straße 126
10179 Berlin-Mitte
psm-gallery.com

Gorki Apartments
Weinbergsweg 25
10119 Berlin-Mitte
gorkiapartments.de

Linnen
Eberswalder Straße 35
10437 Berlin-Prenzlauer Berg
linnenberlin.com

SWEET HOME BERLIN

Michelberger Hotel
Warschauer Straße 39-40
10243 Berlin-Friedrichshain
michelbergerhotel.com

An Hotels mangelt es in dieser Stadt wahrlich nicht. Wer seine Gäste einzigartig unterbringen will, wirft einen Blick auf unsere Shortlist der Lieblingsdomizile. Hier würden sogar Berliner wie wir gerne für ein paar Tage und Nächte unterkommen.

There's certainly no lack of hotels in this city, but if you're looking for a truly unique stay for yourself or that special someone – look no further. Here is our Berlin accommodations shortlist; places were even locals would happily spend a few nights for a lovely staycation!

Hüttenpalast
Hobrechtstraße 65-66
12047 Berlin-Neukölln
huettenpalast.de

Tautes Heim
tautes-heim.de

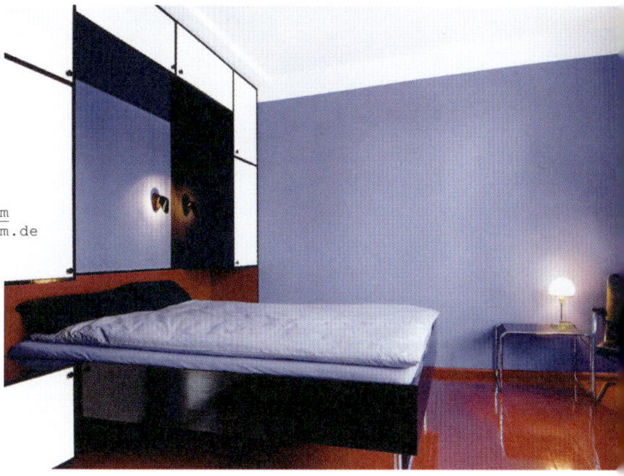

Modern Houseboat
Gustav-Holzmann-Straße 10
10317 Berlin-Rummelsburg
welcomebeyond.com/property/modern-boat

Karlito Apartments
Linienstraße 60
10119 Berlin-Mitte
karlito-apartments.de

BLUE SKY

MIT SONNE IST ALLES BESSER IN BERLIN. ALLES. DAS IST NICHT DAS BLAUE VOM HIMMEL VERSPROCHEN, SONDERN EIN LEITMOTIV. FÜR GLANZVOLLE TAGE UND LANGE ABENDE. WHEN THE CLOUDS BREAK AND THE SUN SHINES, EVERYTHING IN BERLIN FEELS BETTER. DON'T LET CHOICES CONFUSE YOU, WE KNOW JUST THE RIGHT SPOTS TO ENJOY A DAY LIKE THIS.

WO SICH MITTE ZUM BADEN TRIFFT WHERE MITTE MEETS TO TAKE A DIP

Berlin ist von unzähligen Seen umgeben. Über 3000 sollen es sein. Kein Wunder, gibt es doch jeden Sommer große Geheimniskrämerei um den Besten der vielen. Und am Ende trifft man dann doch die ganze Nachbarschaft am „geheimen" Spot – weil Leute wie wir darüber schreiben ... Im Jahr 2013 war der See des Sommers eindeutig der Bernsteinsee und 2014 hat sich daran nichts geändert. Am besten hält man sich auf seiner südlichen Seite auf; das Auto parkt man am Straßenrand. Rund 20 Minuten Fußmarsch führen durch einen schönen Pinienwald, bis man auf die weniger erschlossene „Wildseite" stößt. Hier gibt es, im Gegensatz zu den meisten Seen im Umland, einen breiten, weißen Sandstrand. Besonders für Gruppen und Familien ist das angenehm, da es so genügend Platz gibt, alle Handtücher in der Sonne auszubreiten. Vorerst ist der Bernsteinsee mein persönliches Lieblingsgewässer – bis die nächste geheime Badestelle auftaucht. Berlin is surrounded by countless lakes: over 3,000 to be precise. It's no wonder there's a secret hype on the best lake each summer – until you realize that half of your neighborhood is there. Of course, people like us writing about it doesn't help, but you gotta spread the love, right? In 2013, the "it-lake" was definitely Lake Bernstein, and it made its final breakthrough in 2014. Where you want to go is the south side of the lake. Park your car on the road and walk through a beautiful pine forest for 20 minutes before hitting the lake on its less developed "wild side." It's one of those rare lakes with large white sandy beaches, perfect for big groups and families; there's plenty of space to spread your towels and bathe in the sun. For now this is my favorite lake in Brandenburg, until the next secret spot is discovered.

Text: Sven Hausherr / Photos: Karolina Rosina

Bernsteinsee
16348 Marienwerder
About a 1-hour drive north of Berlin-Mitte

Im Sommer nur wochentags zu empfehlen: der Liepnitzsee nördlich der Stadtgrenze – ein typischer See im Berliner Umland mit rauen Ufern, vielen romantischen Fleckchen und kristallklarem Wasser.

Recommended on weekdays during summer: Liepnitzsee in the north of Berlin, a typical lake in this area with natural rugged shores, crystal clear water, and plenty of hidden nooks for romantic cuddles.

CEE CEE'S GUEST: MARTIN BEHNKE

Als Kreuzberg noch ein gefährliches Pflaster war und das Engelbecken nicht im Zentrum, sondern im Todesstreifen lag, verbrachte Martin seine Kindheit im uncoolen Teil von Mitte – in den Wohnblocks im Heinrich-Heine-Viertel. Nach Stationen im Osten und Süden Deutschlands kam er zurück und lebt jetzt in Kreuzberg. Genauer gesagt neben dem Moviemento Kino und damit in jenem Kiez, den er als Kind fürchtete. Kreuzberg ist für ihn heute „trotz allem berechtigten Gentrifizierungsgejammer noch immer einer der lebenswertesten Orte Deutschlands, an dem es vor allem nicht so schrecklich deutsch zugeht". Neben der Vielzahl an Programmkinos und der Tatsache, dass zwischen dem Schlesischen Tor und Hermannplatz die halbe deutsche Filmbranche zu Hause ist, gibt es einen weiteren Grund, als Drehbuchautor hier zu leben: die vielen Cafés! Dort lassen sich nicht nur filmreife Szenen beobachten, sondern auch niederschreiben. Ob für ein Politdrama, einen Kinderanimationsfilm oder eine Ganoven-Farce über Waffenfanatiker, die er zusammen mit dem tschechischen Autor Jaroslav Rudiš geschrieben hat. Dabei beobachten kann man ihn auf der Sonnenterrasse: im Café Gipfeltreffen. At a time when Kreuzberg was known as a dangerous place and the Engelbecken was not located in the city center but in Berlin's death strip, Martin spent his childhood in the uncool part of Mitte – in the prefab apartment buildings in the Heinrich Heine quarter. After spending some time in other parts of Germany, the screenwriter returned to Berlin and moved right next to the Moviemento cinema in Kreuzberg: the neighborhood he had feared as a child. For Martin, Kreuzberg – despite all the justified complaints about gentrification – remains the only place not as "German" as the rest of the country. Besides the countless movie theaters and the fact that half of Germany's film industry lives between Schlesisches Tor and Hermannplatz, there is another reason why you should chose this neighborhood to live in as a screenwriter: there are loads of cafés! Not only will you witness incidences, which seem like something straight out of a movie at these spots, but you can work on your own script too – whether it's a political drama, a children's film, or a gangster farce produced in collaboration with Czech author Jaroslav Rudiš. You can spot him working on the sunny deck at Café Gipfeltreffen.

agenturhomebase.de

Auf einen Teller Shakshuka und andere israelische Köstlichkeiten geht's ins Devil's Kitchen in der Graefestraße 11. For a dish of shakshuka or other Israeli delicacies, visit Devil's Kitchen at Graefestraße 11.

MARTIN BEHNKE EMPFIEHLT: CAFÉ GIPFELTREFFEN

MARTIN BEHNKE RECOMMENDS: CAFÉ GIPFELTREFFEN

Betritt man das Gipfeltreffen am Görlitzer Park, fühlt man sich, als ob man in die gute Stube von Freunden käme. Nicht nur die bemerkenswerte Anzahl an Stammgästen ist ein sicheres Zeichen dafür, dass man hier ein hervorragendes zweites Zuhause finden kann. Auch hat es erhebliche Vorzüge gegenüber dem eigenen: Man kann in Ruhe arbeiten, das Frühstück ist liebevoll angerichtet und von besten Zutaten. Nebst warmen Schrippen sucht der Kaffee im Umkreis seinesgleichen und die angenehm uneinheitliche Einrichtung aus Holzmöbeln und Kaminofen strahlt unaufdringliche Wärme und Herzlichkeit aus. Genau wie das unglaublich freundliche Personal. Daher fühlt man sich nach einem Besuch im Gipfeltreffen immer etwas besser als zuvor. Wenn das Wetter gut ist, kann man den ganzen Tag auf dem Freisitz in der Sonne verbringen. Neuerdings gibt es auch erstklassiges Abendessen, bei dem man sich durch die erlesene Weinkarte trinken und mit den anderen Stammgästen anfreunden kann. Entering Gipfeltreffen at Görlitzer Park feels like coming to your best friend's home. The astounding amount of regulars may be read as an infallible sign that you've found your perfect second home here. In addition, it comes with some advantages to your own home: you can work calmly, breakfast is caringly prepared with the best ingredients, and the warm rolls and coffee are without equal in the vicinity. Their comforting and eclectic wooden furniture together with the furnace add to the subtle warmth and cordiality of the place, as does the incredibly friendly staff. You will feel better than before, each time you leave Gipfeltreffen. On bright days you can enjoy the sunshine in front of the café all day long. Coming for dinner is an excellent opportunity to try the small yet exquisite wine menu and to meet the other regulars.

Text: Martin Behnke / Photos: Marta Greber

Gipfeltreffen
Görlitzer Straße 68, 10997 Berlin-Kreuzberg
Mon-Fri 9:00-24:00, Sat&Sun 10:00-24:00
gipfeltreffen-kreuzberg.de

SOMMER FÜR EINEN MOMENT
AN ICE-COLD SUMMER MOMENT

Sommer – was gibt es Besseres als Eis am Stiel? Der Popsicle-Trend aus den USA hat Berlin in den letzten Jahren erobert. Immer öfter findet man hausgemachtes Eis am Holzstiel in den Kühltruhen der Stadt. Die Kreationen von Paletas werden in Friedrichshain hergestellt und beeindrucken mit intensivem Geschmack. Die Zutaten: vorwiegend regionales Obst und Gemüse, keinerlei Zusatzstoffe. Unsere Favoriten sind Gurke-Zitrone und Joghurt-Himbeere. Zu kaufen gibt's die Eissorten auf diversen Wochen- und Flohmärkten; wo genau, steht auf der Webseite. Für die nächste Sommerparty kann man das Paletas-Team auch fürs Catering buchen. Yes, summer does actually come to Berlin. And what could be better than an ice-cold popsicle? The American trend landed in Berlin a few years ago and the homemade-popsicle biz only continues to grow. Straight out of Friedrichshain comes Paletas, super delicious ice pops in various combinations. Made only from fresh local fruits, vegetables, and water: no additives. We are all blown away by their intense flavor. Our favorites are cucumber-lemon and yogurt-raspberry. Look out for the Paletas booth at various flea markets or check their website to see where they might pop up next. Also ask them about catering: I'm sure your guests would appreciate this special treat.

Anderer Kiez, andere Geschmacksrichtungen, genauso lecker: die Popsicles vom Fahrradshop Standert in der Invalidenstraße 157 in Mitte. Another neighborhood, different flavors, but just as tasty: the popsicles from the bike shop Standert at Invalidenstraße 157 in Mitte.

Text: Sven Hausherr

Paletas
paletas-berlin.com

RAUS AUFS LAND – ZUR ERHOLUNG INS GÄSTEHAUS NACH LYCHEN

REST & RELAX – IN A COUNTRY-SIDE GUEST HOUSE

Ein echter Berliner verlässt seinen Kiez niemals, heißt es. Wahrscheinlich weil er weiß: Wählt man das richtige Fleckchen außerhalb der Stadt, will man gar nicht mehr zurück. Ein solcher Ort ist Lychen in der Uckermark. Hier, in einer kleinen Inselstadt umgeben von sieben Seen, haben ein neuseeländischer Künstler und seine deutsche Frau, eine Architektin, eine Enklave des guten Geschmacks und formvollendeter ländlicher Erholung geschaffen. Die passt noch dazu ins Budget eines jeden unterbeschäftigten Performancekünstlers. In jahrelanger Arbeit hat das Paar das ehemalige Lychener Gerichtshaus in eine gemütliche Herberge verwandelt, inklusive liebevoll restaurierter Findlings-Möbel aus Omas Zeiten. Hinzu kommt das leckere Frühstück, der Seeblick aus den Zimmern, das griffbereite Boot und die Tatsache, dass man vom Kuckuck geweckt wird - statt von zankenden Pub-Crawlern. Genügend Argumente, im Sommer mal rauszukommen. According to the old adage, real Berliners never leave their Kiez. I wonder if they know that it is so beautiful out there that they will hardly be able to bring themselves back to their "Kiez." Take, for instance, the Uckermark town of Lychen. Surrounded by seven lakes, a New Zealand artist and his architect wife have created the perfect country retreat, a little enclave of good taste that should fit the budget of even the least commercially successful performance artist. It took the couple a few years of painstaking work to transform the former Lychen courthouse into a beautiful bed and breakfast, complete with lovingly restored heirloom furniture. Combine that with the lake view, the yummy breakfast, the relaxing garden, the ready-to-use canoes, and being gently woken by a cuckoo instead of squabbling pub-crawlers; there are very few reasons left not to get out there in summer.

Text: Viviane Stappmanns

Lychen House
Kirchstraße 3, 17279 Lychen
lychenhouse.de

Die Uckermark in der Flasche für die Erholung zwischendurch? Kann man bestellen: auf wild-kraeuter.com als grüne Säfte und Smoothies.
Uckermark in a bottle? Order green juices and smoothies at wild-kraeuter.com for your daily dose of well-being.

Sehr zu empfehlen ist auch Mmaah am Columbiadamm 160 in Neukölln – der auf koreanisches BBQ spezialisierte Imbiss der koreanisch-deutschen Brüder Andreas und Sebastian. Mmaah at Columbiadamm 160 in Neukölln also specializes in Korean BBQ. It is run by two half-Korean, half-German brothers, Andreas and Sebastian. Highly recommended!

STREET FOOD AUF KOREANISCH
KOREAN STREET FOOD IN A SHACK

„‚Ban Ban' ist Koreanisch und bedeutet halb und halb", erklärt Linh Vu, die den gleichnamigen kleinen Imbiss gemeinsam mit Mark Roh betreibt. Der Name steht für die vietnamesischen und koreanischen Elemente, die sich in den Gerichten wiederfinden. Denn Linh ist Halbvietnamesin, Mark Halbkoreaner. Während des Architekturstudiums haben sich die beiden kennengelernt, viel gemeinsam gekocht und schließlich den Traum vom eigenen Imbiss wahr werden lassen. Die Basis der meisten Gerichte bildet koreanisches BBQ, kombiniert wird es ganz unterschiedlich: Der „Bulgogi Beef Burger" kommt mit Kimchi, hausgemachter Mayonnaise und Salat auf den Teller. Seit kurzem kreiert Sterne-Patissier Andreas Israelewski die passenden Desserts – zum Beispiel Kokos-Limetten-Pannacotta mit Chili-Ingwer-Mango. Just walk right up to the brightly colored shack on Hermannstraße, past kebab shops and bakeries, for some hearty Korean soul food – because this is where Ban Ban Kitchen is at. "In Korean 'Ban Ban' literally means half-half," explains Linh Vu, who runs the restaurant together with Mark Roh. The name refers to the fact that their dishes contain both Vietnamese and Korean elements; Linh is half Vietnamese and Mark is half Korean. They met while studying architecture, started cooking together, and came up with their dream of owning a fast food restaurant. "We designed everything here ourselves and had friends help implement them," said Linh. While Korean BBQ is the basis of most dishes, there are various combinations. The bulgogi beef burger, for example, comes with kimchi, homemade mayonnaise, and a salad. Star pastry chef Andreas Israelewski recently started making matching desserts like coconut lime panna cotta with chili-ginger-mango.

Text: Laura Storfner / Photo: Tobias Faisst

<u>Ban Ban Kitchen</u>
Hermannstraße 205, 12049 Berlin-Neukölln
Mon, Tue&Thu 17:00-22:00, Fri&Sat 17:00-23:00, Sun 16:00-22:00

DIE SONNENTERRASSE AM VERWUNSCHENEN FRIEDHOF
SUN-DRENCHED CAFÉ IN AN ENCHANTED CEMETERY

Das Café Strauss am Friedrichswerderschen Friedhof an der Bergmannstraße ist ein Juwel! Seit 2013 röstet Besitzerin Olga Strauss dort ihren eigenen Kaffee. Die Heißluftröstmaschine steht gleich neben dem Eingang. Während man seinen Kaffee trinkt, ein Stück Kuchen oder eine Stulle isst, kann man den Bohnen beim Auf- und Abhüpfen und Dunklerwerden zusehen, bis es schließlich im ganzen Raum köstlich duftet. Wenn ab Mittag die Sonne auf die gemütliche Terrasse der ehemaligen Aufbahrungshalle scheint, vergisst man beinahe, dass man am Rand eines Friedhofs sitzt. Wer Zeit hat, schließt einen Spaziergang auf dem riesigen, verwunschenen Gelände an. The beautiful terrace of Café Strauss at the Friedrichswerderscher Cemetery is an ideal spot to enjoy the sun peacefully and quietly. With the hot air roasting machine right next to the door, owner Olga Strauss has been roasting her signature coffee here since 2013. While enjoying a cup of coffee and a piece of cake, or a German "Stulle" (open sandwich) you can watch the beans bounce around and darken until the room is filled with a delicious scent. In the afternoon, when the sun hits the cozy terrace of the former funeral hall, you almost forget about the fact that you're on cemetery grounds. Taking a stroll on the enchanted premises, it's easy to obliviate time.

Text: Lorena Simmel / Photos: Sasha Kharchenko

Café Strauss
Bergmannstraße 42, 10961 Berlin-Kreuzberg
Tue-Sun from 9:00
cafestraussberlin.de

Kaffee
STRAUS
KAFFE
THEIERES

Für Trubel und Fundstücke lohnt am Wochenende der Weg entlang der Bergmannstraße bis zum Trödelmarkt auf dem Marheinekeplatz.
Follow Bergmannstraße until you reach the Trödelmarkt at Marheinekeplatz, a small flea market on weekends.

Statt Kartoffeln ausgraben: Schätze finden – vom Vintage-Toaster bis zum Teakholztisch. Bei Treibgut, in der Oranienstraße 53, schräg genüber. Instead of digging up potatoes, hunt down great finds across the street in Treibgut at Oranienstraße 53 – you'll find everything from a vintage toaster to a teak table.

MITTAGESSEN ZWISCHEN BEETEN & BÄUMEN LUNCH AMID PLANTING BEDS & TREES

„Erntereif", steht auf einem Schild am Gitterzaun. Darunter eine von Hand geschriebene Liste mit Kräutern und Gemüsesorten, die ich heute in den Prinzessinnengärten ernten kann. Ich gehe durch das Eingangstor und stehe inmitten von bepflanzten Kästen und mit Erde gefüllten Säcken. Der laute, hektische Moritzplatz ist nur wenige Schritte entfernt, gefühlt aber Welten, und hier ganz schnell vergessen. Statt Gemüse aus der Erde zu holen gehe ich ein paar Schritte weiter, nehme auf einer der vielen Sitzgelegenheiten Platz. Über mir in den Bäumen Lichterketten und auf dem Tisch alsbald das Mittagessen. Köstlich zubereitet mit regionalen Zutaten aus ökologischem Anbau, vieles davon aus diesem urbanen Garten selbst. Ein Ort der Entschleunigung im trubeligen Berlin und ein sehr erholsamer Lunch-Spot! "Ready for harvesting" reads a little sign on the lattice fence. Below is a handwritten list of herbs and vegetables ready to pick. I enter and find myself in the midst of boxes with sacks of soil. Just a few steps from hectic Moritzplatz - but the traffic feels far away. Instead of fetching vegetables from the ground, I sit down in the garden dining area where strings of light hang in the trees above. My lunch quickly appears on the table in front of me: a yummy organic dish made with regional ingredients, some of which were even harvested in this urban garden. This spot allows you to slow down and enjoy the calm away from the hustle and bustle of Berlin. One of my favorite lunch spots!

Text: Karolina Rosina / Photos: Marta Greber

Prinzessinnengärten
Prinzenstraße 35-38, 10969 Berlin-Kreuzberg
Apr-Oct 11:00-18:00; Garden Café 12:00-22:00, Lunch 12:00-15:00
prinzessinnengarten.net

GREY SKY

DER HERBST IST ERTRÄGLICH, ABER KURZ. DER WINTER DAS GEGENTEIL. ZWISCHEN OKTOBER UND MÄRZ ALSO BESSER ZU HAUSE BLEIBEN. NOTFALLPLAN GEGEN DAS FACETTENREICHE BERLINER GRAU? GEMÜTLICHKEIT. IF YOU CAN'T HANDLE THE GLOOM, DON'T MOVE TO BERLIN IN THE WINTER. BETTER YET, DON'T BOTHER VISITING. OUR KEY TO SURVIVAL IS EMBRACING THE COZY.

GEHOBENE TEEKULTUR & FEINE PAPETERIE A PLACE FOR DEDICATED TEA LOVERS

Unweit des Savignyplatzes bietet P&T feine Tees aus aller Welt. Das aparte Geschäft, designt von Fabian von Ferrari, ist aber mehr als nur ein schöner Teeladen. Es ist ein Ort der Vermittlung von Tee und Teekultur. Im vorderen Raum zeigt Gründer Jens de Gruyter seine Selektion nach Oxidationsgrad sortiert. Alle Sorten werden in kleinen Schalen präsentiert, so kann man die Blätter betrachten und im Gespräch mehr über deren Anbaugebiete erfahren. Im Rahmen einer Tee-Zeremonie kann die persönliche Auswahl auch direkt vor Ort verkostet werden. Wunderbar gearbeitetes Geschirr, unter anderem aus Taiwan, ergänzt das Konzept, ebenso eine Papeterie-Abteilung mit eleganten Grußkarten, Notizheften und Kleinigkeiten. Unbedingt vorbeischauen und viel Zeit mitbringen. This airy, minimalist space for tea and tea culture was designed by Fabian von Ferrari and opened by founder Jens de Gruyter, who is mad about aromatic leaves. You can see and smell the world’s finest teas here. They are presented on a large table and organized by levels of oxidation. Two tea-tasting stations will help you choose your favorite. The walls are decorated with beautiful teapots and cups, of which many are from Taiwan. The shop also carries a fine selection of stationery goods from all over the world. I recommend visiting the shop when you have plenty of time.

Text: Nina Trippel / Photos: Ludger Paffrath, Emmanuel Decouard

P&T – Paper and Tea
Bleibtreustraße 4, 10623 Berlin-Charlottenburg
Mon-Sat 11:00-18:00
paperandtea.com

P&T bietet ebenfalls eine kleine Auswahl an wunderbaren Produkten von Wednesday Paper Works an; das komplette Angebot findet man online auf: wednesday-paper-works.com. P&T's paper collection includes a fine selection of beautifully designed stationery by Wednesday Paper Works; alternatively, visit the Berlin brand online at wednesday-paper-works.com.

WASSER, WIESEN, WÄLDER – EIN AUSFLUG AN DEN HELLSEE
MEADOWS, WOODS & WATER – A TRIP TO LAKE HELLSEE

Genug vom städtischen Grau? Ab an den Hellsee, denn das ist auch bei eisigen Temperaturen ein schöner Ausflug. Neben Erkundungstouren kann man bei stabilen Minusgraden hier auch Schlittschuhlaufen. Angekommen in Lanke, läuft man bei einem schönen Spaziergang am Schloss vorbei. Man folgt dem alten Wanderweg, der durch den kleinen Schlosspark führt – gestaltet vom berühmten Landschaftsarchitekt Peter Josef Lenné –, und gelangt so direkt zum See. Der Weg an das Ufer führt über weite Wiesen, vorbei an der alten Hellmühle, und dann wieder hinauf in die Erlen- und Buchenwälder, die den See säumen. Perfekt für einen Halb- oder Ganztagesausflug. Fed up with the grey winter cityscape? Then it's time for a trip to Lake Hellsee. It's always pleasant, even on ice-cold days. You will enjoy quiet strolls here in fall and winter. If the temperature stays below zero for a while, you can ice-skate on the lake. Take the lovely path that runs through the small garden of Lanke Castle created by famous landscape architect Peter Josef Lenné, and soon you'll hit the lake. The way to the bank will lead you through the meadows, past the old Hell Mill, and then back to the alder and beech woods framing the lake. Lake Hellsee is the perfect getaway for a mini daytrip.

Text & photos: Milena Kalojanov

Hellsee
16348 Wandlitz-Lanke
Head north on the autobahn A11 from Berlin, exit at Lanke

Kostenlos Eislaufen kann man bei entsprechenden Temperaturen in Kreuzberg auf dem Engelbecken am Michaelkirchplatz in Kreuzberg. For free ice-skating in the city, head to Engelbecken at Michaelkirchplatz in Kreuzberg.

KAFFEETRINKEN IM GLASHAUS
COFFEE IN A GLASSHOUSE

Für einen Besuch im Café in der Gartenakademie hat sich die Reise bis nach Dahlem gelohnt. Für mich ist es eines der schönsten Cafés in ganz Berlin. Man betritt die in einem Glashaus gelegenen Räumlichkeiten durch einen mit Blumen und Pflanzen gesäumten, langen Gang. Am hinteren Ende kann man dann – ebenfalls umgeben von vielen Pflanzen – einen Kaffee trinken, etwas essen und dabei ein Lichtbad nehmen; ideal für Wintertage, wenn man ständig auf der Jagd nach ein paar Sonnenstrahlen ist. Auch an Regentagen oder wenn der Schnee leise aufs Dach rieselt ist das Café ein wunderbarer Ort für ein romantisches Treffen. The café at the Garden Academy is definitely worth the trip to Dahlem. This botanical coffee shop is one of the most beautiful and romantic spots in Berlin, located inside of a glasshouse. Enter through a beautiful arcade full of orchids and plants, and you'll find the sun-drenched café all the way in the back, surrounded by glass walls and flowers. This café is perfect for winter, when catching a little bit of sun becomes somewhat of a hunt. The place can easily turn into the most perfect setting for a romantic date on a rainy day or with soft snow falling onto the glass ceilings.

Text: Sven Hausherr / Photos: Marta Greber

Das Café in der Gartenakademie
Altensteinstraße 15a, 14195 Berlin-Dahlem
Apr-Sep: Mon-Sat 10:00-19:00, Sun 10:00-16:00
Oct-Mar: Mon-Fri 11:00-17:30, Sat 10:00-17:30, Sun 10:00-17:00
dascafeindergartenakademie.de

Kreuzberger Tage und Nächte sind lang in der Dresdener Straße: Im Café Dresden trifft man sich zum Frühstück, im Mercosy zum koreanischen Lunch und in der Cevicheria zum Abendessen. Zur Filmstunde geht's in Kino Babylon und auf einen Absacker ins Möbel Olfe.

Kreuzberg days and nights are long on Dresdener Straße: start your day with breakfast at Café Dresden. Try a Korean-inspired lunch at Mercosy. Enjoy dinner at Cevicheria, then it's movie time at Kino Babylon. Möbel Olfe is where we go for our nightcap.

AUF EINEN DRINK MIT LUIS BUÑUEL HAVE A DRINK WITH LUIS BUÑUEL

Zwei Minuten Fußweg vom Kottbusser Tor entfernt, den Obstständen, Wochenendtouristen und Junkies, wartet eine der stilvollsten Cocktailbars der Stadt: Der Würgeengel. Luis Buñuels Kultfilm „El ángel exterminador" lieh dieser Kreuzberger Institution den Namen. Ein alter Ventilator dreht an der Decke langsam seine Kreise, bordeauxrote Samtbänke ziehen sich an der Wand entlang. Die glasgetäfelte Decke reflektiert das Licht der Kerzen, Stimmengewirr mischt sich mit leiser Soulmusik. Wie jeden Samstag ist die Bar brechend voll, und so sitze ich am dunklen Holztresen, unterhalte mich mit dem Barkeeper, der sein Handwerk par excellence beherrscht, und trinke einen Martini-Cocktail. Wenn man irgendwann dem unerklärlichen Buñuelschen Zwang widerstehen kann und die Bar verlässt, erscheint es fast surreal, wieder auf der Dresdener Straße zu stehen. Just a two-minute walk from busy Kottbusser Tor with all its fruit vendors, weekend tourists, and junkies you'll find one of the city's most exquisite cocktail bars: The Würgeengel. This Kreuzberg institution was named after Luis Buñuel's film "El ángel exterminador." An old ceiling fan spins slowly and burgundy-colored velvet banquettes stretch along the wall. Candlelights reflect on the mirrored ceiling. Voices mix with quiet soul music. Almost every Saturday I find myself sitting at the counter, sipping a martini and talking to the bartender who is a master of his trade. If you manage to resist the inexplicable Buñuel-like compulsion to stay and actually leave the bar, it will feel pretty surreal to be back on Dresdener Straße again.

Text: Laura Storfner / Photos: Peter Meffert

Würgeengel
Dresdener Straße 122, 10999 Berlin-Kreuzberg
Daily 19:00 till late
wuergeengel.de

WINTERPARTIE IM WEDDING: AUF ZUM SCHLITTELN! WINTER WONDERLAND: SLEDDING IN WEDDING!

Mit einem Schlitten einen verschneiten Hügel hinuntersausen ist ohne Frage eine der amüsantesten Aktivitäten im Winter. In Berlin ist es zwar nicht ganz einfach, einen geeigneten Hang zu finden, aber es gibt sie: die kleinen Erhebungen. Für Kids und Junggebliebene. Zum Beispiel im Volkspark Rehberge im Wedding. Hier führt eine kleine Schneise durch den Mini-Wald. Wenn Wetter- und Schneelage es erlauben, kann man immerhin 300 bis 400 Meter den Hügel hinabschlitteln. Going down a hill on a sled is undoubtedly a fun winter staple, but it’s not easy to find a real slope in Berlin. There are a few decent ones, however, especially for kids and for the young at heart. I like the Volkspark Rehberge in Wedding because it feels secluded. With a long, wide slope cutting through the woods, you can actually ride for 300-400 meters.

Text: Sven Hausherr / Photos: Martin Mascheski

Volkspark Rehberge
Windhuker Straße 52A, 13351 Berlin-Wedding

Statt bergab geradeaus: Langlauf-Anhänger treffen sich bei Schnee auf der Tempelhofer Freiheit. Instead of downhill, straight across: on days with good snow conditions, cross-country skiers meet at Tempelhofer Freiheit park.

EIN ENTSPANNTER START INS NEUE JAHR IN BAD SAAROW

RELAX INTO THE NEW YEAR AT BAD SAAROW

Der Januar ist der perfekte Monat für ein heißes Bad und der ideale Zeitpunkt, sich nach den Feiertagen und Feiergelagen zu erholen. Etwa in Bad Saarow, circa eine Stunde östlich von Berlin – einfach zu erreichen mit der Bahn oder dem Auto. Hier kann man einen Tag in der Therme verbringen und in einem Außenbecken im warmen Quellwasser baden. Dann einen Spaziergang entlang des Scharmützelsees und durch die Natur anschließen – gute Landluft garantiert. January is the perfect month for soaking in a hot bath and relaxing after the post-holiday come down. Bad Saarow is about one hour east of Berlin and easy to reach by car or train. Swimming in the warm outdoor mineral water pool is truly an amazing experience, especially in the middle of winter when the air is chilly and crisp. The pool is right next to a lake, so weather permitting, we recommend taking a walk afterwards and enjoying a breath of fresh air in the countryside before returning to the city.

Text: Sven Hausherr

SaarowTherme
Am Kurpark 1, 15526 Bad Saarow
Daily 9:00-21:00
therme.bad-saarow.de

Eine Oase der Entspannung mitten im Kiez? Das Stadtbad Neukölln in der Ganghoferstraße 3 bietet u.a. eine finnische Sauna und ein griechisch-römisches Dampfbad in denkmalgeschütztem Ambiente.
Looking for a place to relax in the city center? The amazing Stadtbad Neukölln (public pool) at Ganghoferstraße 3 has a Finnish sauna and a Greco-Roman steam bath.

GEMÜTLICHKEIT MIT FRANZÖSISCHEM AKZENT
COZYNESS WITH A FRENCH ACCENT

Wer eine Reise nach Frankreich plant, kann sich in diesem Café wunderbar darauf einstimmen. Köstliche Croissants, kaltes Frühstück mit Tarte oder Quiche, Kuchen nach französischen Original-Rezepten und guter Kaffee stehen auf der Karte. Vintage-Möbel sorgen für die behagliche Atmosphäre, zusammengetragen von den freundlichen Inhaber-Geschwistern Carole und Eric, die ein Händchen für Einrichtung haben und ihre Gäste mit sympathischem Akzent willkommen heißen. Das Louise Chérie ist ein Stück Paris in Berlin. If you're planning a trip to France, this is a good place to start. They serve delicious croissants, beautiful cakes baked according to traditional French recipes, cold breakfasts served with a slice of tart or quiche, and of course good coffee. The place has a unique ambience thanks to the wooden vintage furniture collected from all over Berlin, and an eye for detail. The very friendly staff, including a French brother and sister with very charming accents, make you feel immediately comfortable and welcome. You can easily say that the Louise Chérie Café is a little piece of Paris in Berlin.

Text & photos: Marta Greber

Louise Chérie Café
Grünberger Straße 91, 10245 Berlin-Friedrichshain
Wed-Mon 10:00-19:00
louisecheriecafe.de

Die besten handgemachten Croissants gibt es bei Les Pâtisseries de Sébastien auf der Invalidenstraße 157 in Mitte. You'll find the best homemade croissants at Les Pâtisseries de Sébastien at Invalidenstraße 157 in Mitte.

BORN & BRED

DEM LOKALPATRIOTISMUS GESCHMACKVOLL AUSDRUCK ZU VERLEIHEN IST MÖGLICH. MIT BERLINER BRILLEN, BROTSORTEN ODER BUCHSTABEN. IDEEN GEDEIHEN IN ALLEN BEZIRKEN. THIS CITY IS ALWAYS CREATING SOMETHING NEW AND EXCITING. SO MANY THINGS ARE AUTHENTICALLY BERLIN: FROM FASHION TO BREAD TO FONTS TO SPECS.

DAS UNIVERSUM DER BERLINER MODE BERLIN FASHION UNITE

Was das Etikett „Berliner Mode" wirklich bedeutet, kann man nicht theoretisch erfassen – man muss es mit eigenen Augen sehen und am eigenen Körper spüren. Das geht im Konk. Seit 2012 geleitet von Edda Mann, führt dieses sorgsam kuratierte Geschäft Mode, Schmuck und Accessoires, die in der deutschen Hauptstadt entstehen. Hier wird klar, dass die Szene so divers wie kosmopolitisch ist. Filigraner Schmuck der Japanerin und Wahl-Berlinerin Naoko Ogawa sowie Holzschuhe von Anntian sind auf den Präsentationskuben arrangiert. Auch auf den Kleiderstangen findet man die eigenwilligen, aber wunderbar poetischen Entwürfe von Anntian, die vor allem außerhalb Deutschlands überaus erfolgreich sind. Die mutigen Strickkreationen von Boessert/Schorn enthüllen erst beim näheren Betrachten und Befühlen ihre Komplexität. In den großzügigen Umkleidekabinen hat man Zeit und Raum, sich den Entwürfen anzunähern, und Edda und ihr Team erklären liebenswürdig und bereitwillig, welches Label wie und wo produziert wird. Bei einem der vielen Shop-Events kann man die Designer auch selbst kennenlernen. Wer eine Prise Berliner Stil in die Welt tragen oder junge Labels entdecken möchte, sollte Konk bei seiner Shoppingroute unbedingt mit einplanen. Berlin fashion: no words capture exactly what this means. You have to see it with your own eyes and feel it with your own body. Konk is a great place to start. Since 2012, Edda Mann has been showcasing a carefully curated selection of Berlin-made fashion, jewelry, and accessories. At Konk, it becomes clear that the scene is as diverse as it is cosmopolitan. Filigree jewelry by Japanese Berlin-based designer Naoko Ogawa is arranged alongside presentation cubes featuring massive wooden shoes by Anntian. Anntian's idiosyncratic and wonderfully poetic garments can be found on the clothes racks – the label is über-successful, especially outside of Germany. The complexity of Boessert/Schorn's bold knitwear creations emerges only upon closer examination. In the spacious changing rooms you can take your time and revel in the experience of trying on new designs. Edda and her team enjoy telling you about the labels and where they are produced. If you want to meet one of the designers, stop by one of their many in-store events. To discover and take home young fashion made in the capital city of Germany.

Text: Nina Trippel / Photos: Achim Hatzius, Gabriel Braun

Konk
Kleine Hamburger Straße 15, 10117 Berlin-Mitte
Mon-Fri 12:00-19:00, Sat 12:00-18:00
konk-berlin.de

Führt auch Design aus Berlin: École Boutique in der Torstraße 3. Hier findet man u.a. Mode von Isabell de Hillerin oder Schmuck von Kjeld. École Boutique at Torstraße 3 also carries Berlin fashion, including apparel by Isabell de Hillerin as well as jewelry by Kjeld.

FÜNF MODELLE, EINE VISION

FIVE FRAMES, ONE VISION

Schuhe, E-Mail-Adressen, Unterhosen – von manchen Dingen sollte man mehr als ein Exemplar besitzen. Bei Brillen hat es sich bisher anders verhalten: Brillenträger verschmolzen mit ihren Gestellen. Bisweilen erschrak man morgens beim Anblick eines nacktmullartigen Wesens ohne dessen formgebende Sehhilfe. David Kamp beweist mit seinem Brillenlabel Owl Optics, dass dem nicht so sein muss. Die schlichten aber schicken Modelle sind durchnummeriert von „Eins" bis „Fünf" und in jeweils fünf Farben erhältlich, z.B. im eigenen Onlineshop. Pro Gestell, inklusive Korrekturgläser, macht der Unternehmer Brillenträger mit einem Preis von 150 Euro glücklich, aber nicht arm.

Shoes, email addresses, underwear – of some things you simply need more than one. When it comes to spectacles, however, it was different until now: people used to be permanently attached to their only pair of frames and without them you'd think that a naked mole rat was sleeping next to you. Luckily, David Kamp demonstrates that this no longer needs to be the case. Their Berlin-based brand Owl Optics offers a set of five different frames, aptly called "Eins" to "Fünf," which come in five different shades. The frames are available in his online shop. Priced at €150 (including corrective lenses), they are bound to make spectacle wearers happy and not send them to the poorhouse.

Text: Sarah Weinknecht / Photos: Kira Bunse, Jonas Lindström

Owl
owloptics.com

Wer hier nicht fündig wird: Lunettes in der Torstraße 172 in Mitte hält eine Auswahl an Vintage-Brillen bereit und die Schwester-Boutique in der Dunckerstraße 18 in Prenzlauer Berg sogar Kinderbrillen. If you can't find what you're looking for, just head to Lunettes at Torstraße 172 in Mitte. The store carries vintage glasses and its sister boutique at Dunckerstraße 18 in Prenzlauer Berg even sells stylish children's glasses.

WO DESIGN, MODE & KUNST SICH TREFFEN WHERE FASHION MEETS ART& DESIGN

Das Kollektiv aus Künstlern und Designern rund um die beiden UdK-Absolventinnen Magdalena Kohler und Miriam Lehnart nennt sich Staub. Ihr Shop-Atelier ist jedoch das Gegenteil von Muff: Hier findet man Mode von Köhlers Männerlabel August, Schmuck und Objekte von Freunden und Kollegen und schöne Dinge aus aller Welt. Antreffen kann man die Macher des Öfteren vor Ort und bei ihren Ausstellungen und Partys. University of the Arts graduates Magdalena Kohler and Miriam Lehnart and a collective of arround ten artists and designers call themselves Staub – "dust" in English. But their shop and studio is anything but musty – you'll find fashion from Köhler's menswear label August, jewelry by friends and colleagues, and cool things from all over the world. You can often meet the designers in the store or chat with them during their many exhibitions and parties.

Text: Nina Trippel

Staub Shop & Studio
Manteuffelstraße 48, 10999 Berlin-Kreuzberg
Wed-Sat 12:00-19:00
staubshop.com

CEE CEE'S GUEST: AILINE LIEFELD

Mit Ailine Liefeld in den Tag starten ist einfach: Auf Instagram kann man mit ihr gemeinsam vom 13. Stock über die Stadt schauen. Oder direkt auf den Frühstücksteller. Die erste Mahlzeit des Tages ist ihr die Liebste, lässt sie verlauten. Kein Wunder, schmeckt Berlin für sie doch „wie ein richtig gutes Katerfrühstück". Auch für die Folgemahlzeiten des Tages kann sich die gebürtige „Randberlinerin" begeistern. Genaue Einblicke und Ansichten ihres kulinarischen Könnens gibt sie auf aicuisne.com, um „die Schönheit und Einfachheit des Kochens mit anderen zu teilen". Ihr Blog zählt zu den bekanntesten seiner Art in Deutschland, und das könnte daran liegen, dass Ailine exzellenten Geschmack hat. Nicht nur bei der Komposition im Kochtopf, sondern auch beim Arrangement auf dem Teller. Als Fotografin hält sie ihre Kreationen für alle Hungrigen auch in Bildern fest – ob Ofenschlupfer, Steak-Sandwich oder türkischen Toast. Die Inspiration bringt sie von ihren vielen Reisen mit. Brot spielt oft eine zentrale Rolle. Wer nicht nur ihre Rezepte nachkochen, sondern auch wissen will, wo sie ihre Lieblingslebensmittel herbekommt, sollte umblättern: Für Cee Cee hat sie Berlins beste Bäckerei besucht. You can start each day with Ailine Liefeld: she shares her view of the city from the 13th floor or her breakfast plate via Instagram. She claims that the first meal of the day is her favorite. This comes as no surprise since Berlin tastes like "a really great hangover breakfast" to Ailine. However, she knows how to enjoy the rest of the day's meals as well. "In order to share the beauty and simplicity of cooking with others," she offers insights into her culinary expertise on aicuisine.com – one of the most successful and authentic food blogs in Germany. The reason for her success may be that she has fantastic taste. Not only when it comes to the ingredients she combines in a saucepan, but also with regard to the way the food is arranged on a plate. As a photographer, she also takes pictures of her food creations, capturing them for all hungry folks – whether it's pastries, steak sandwiches, or Turkish toast. She draws inspiration from her many trips around the world, and bread often plays a very important role. If her recipes aren't the only thing you want to try, turn to the next page and you can pick up one of her favorite groceries too. For Cee Cee, Ailine visited Berlin's best bakery. →

aicuisine.com
instagram.com/aicuisine

AILINE LIEFELD EMPFIEHLT: SOLUNA BROT & OEL AILINE LIEFELD RECOMMENDS: SOLUNA BROT & OEL

Als Peter Klann, der Geschäftsführer von Soluna Brot & Oel, meiner Anfrage entsprach, hinter die Kulissen seines Betriebes schauen zu dürfen, war es um mich geschehen! Zu lange schon bin ich Fan dieser Bäckerei, bei der man die vermutlich besten Sauerteigbrote Berlins bekommt. Viel zu rar sind sie ohnehin – die echten Bäckereien. Besonders schön bei Soluna ist der große Steinofen im vorderen Teil des Ladenlokals, in dem das Brot tatsächlich noch gebacken wird. Zu kaufen gibt es vom klassischen Sauerteigbrot über Brotchips bis zu Ciabatta alles, was das Herz begehrt. Eine Spezialität ist der Rundling, ein zwei Kilogramm schweres Roggensauerteigbrot, das auch gut zwei Wochen liegen kann, ohne an Qualität zu verlieren. Überhaupt halten sich alle Backwaren von Soluna viel länger als die der umliegenden Backshops mit ihren tiefgefroren angelieferten Teigrohlingen. Ich würde sogar so weit gehen, die Brote von Soluna Freunden als Geschenk mitzubringen, so außergewöhnlich ist die Qualität. Im Laden gibt es außerdem regionale Käse- und Wurstspezialitäten, den ein oder anderen Brotaufstrich, Öle und andere Leckereien. Wenn die Sonne scheint, laden die Stühle und Tische vor der Tür auch zum Verweilen ein. When Peter Klann agreed to let me take a behind-the-scenes look at his bakery, I was walking on air. I'd been a fan of Soluna for a long time, since this is where you find the best sourdough bread in Berlin; fine bakeries are a rare commodity here. Upon entering the premises, you'll see a huge stone oven that is still being used. On the counter you'll find a variety of baked goods: classic sourdough loaves, bread chips, and ciabatta. The store's specialty is the two kilogram round sourdough rye bread, that is still fresh and edible after two weeks. In general, all the breads at Soluna stay fresh much longer than breads made by other bakeries. That's because Soluna's dough is freshly made; it isn't delivered frozen to the shop. I always bring breads from Soluna when invited to friends – the quality is simply exceptional and my love for it is immense! Regional cheese and cold meat specialties plus a variety of spreads, oils, and other delicious stuff are offered at the store as well. Those with a sweet tooth will enjoy their home-baked cakes. If the sun is out you can enjoy the fine food in their outdoor seating area.

Text & photos: Ailine Liefeld

Soluna Brot & Oel
Gneisenaustraße 58, 10961 Berlin-Kreuzberg
Mon-Fri 10:00-19:00, Sat 8:00-16:00

Für Ailine seit Jahren ungeschlagen der Lieblingsspot zum Lunch: das Dudu auf der Torstraße 134 in Mitte. Nothing rivals lunch at Dudu located at Torstraße 134 in Mitte for Ailine: simply the best.

ABCDEFGHIJKLMNOPQRSTUVWXYZ
abcdefghijklmnopqrstuvwxyzß
0123456789 0123456789 0123456789
ÀÁÂÃÄÅÆĀĂĄẠǺǼÇĆĈĊČĎĐÈÉÊËĒĔĖĘĚĜĞĠĢĤĦ
ŲÌÍÎÏĮĨĪĬĴĶĹĻĽĿŁḾŃŅŇŊÑÒÓÔÕÖØŌŎŐǾỌŒ
ŔŖŘŜŞŠȘŚŤŢŦÙÚÛÜŨŪŬŮŰŲỤẀẂẄẂỲŸŶÝŹŻŽĐÞ
àáâãäåæāăąạǻǽçćĉċčďđèéêëēĕėęěĝğġģĥħ
ĳîìïíįĩīĭĵķĺļľŀłńņňŉŋòóôõöøōŏőǿọœ
ŕŗřŝşšșśťţŧùúûüũūŭůűųụŵẁẃẅýÿŷỳźżžðþſſ
abcdefghijklmnopqrstuvwxyz

¼ ½ ¾ 0123456789/0123456789
¿?¡!.:;…',' ',"",,«»‹›{}()[]|¦\/·•‐–—
&@¥€$£¢¤©®™ªº§¶†‡*
%‰%‰∂πμ√∞∫#+±-–×÷=≈≠◊<>~

BERLINER BUCHSTABEN VON FATYPE BERLIN LETTERS BY FATYPE

Fatype ist eine junge Berliner Typefoundry, die maßgeschneiderte und eigene Schriften gestaltet. Gegründet wurde sie von Yassin Baggar und Anton Koovit im Jahr 2012, nachdem sie gemeinsam für GQ France und Google Schriften entwickelt hatten. Eine ihrer Arbeiten ist die „U8" – eine Sans Serif-Schrift, die ihre Wurzeln in der U-Bahn-Beschriftung der gleichnamigen Linie hat, die Reinickendorf mit Neukölln verbindet. Die Idee dahinter: ein Stück Geschichte zu konservieren und daraus einen ausgereiften Schriftsatz für die zeitgenössische Anwendung zu entwickeln. Verkauft werden die „U8" und weitere Fatype-Schriften im eigenen Onlineshop. Founded by Anton Koovit and Yassin Baggar, Fatype is a new Berlin-based type foundry that specializes in tailor-made fonts and retail typefaces. Anton and Yassin formed Fatype after collaborating on the creation of typefaces for GQ France and Google. One of their releases is the geometric sans serif "U8" – an homage to the old Berlin subway signage, particularly the subway line U8 that connects the northern borough of Reinickendorf with Neukölln in the south. The goal was to restore a piece of history by transforming the individual handcrafted station signage into a formal typeface. The "U8" typeface and their other creations are sold in their online shop.

Text: Sven Hausherr

Fatype
fatype.com

Wer klassische Schriftsätze und ein manuelles Druck-Erzeugnis bevorzugt, für den setzt Heino Fröhlich Bleibuchstaben in Reih und Glied – in Otto Wentzel's Druckerei in der Leibnizstraße 28 in Charlottenburg. If you're looking for classic typesets: Heino Fröhlich will set them for you, letter by letter, at Otto Wentzel's print shop at Leibnizstraße 28 in Charlottenburg.

WOCHENMARKT TRIFFT STREET FOOD EARTHLY PLEASURES MEET COSMOPOLITAN DELICACIES

Die Markthalle Neun ist ein Wochenmarkt mit reicher Geschichte, einzigartigen Veranstaltungen und einer großen Auswahl an fairen, ökologischen und regionalen Produkten. Sie wurde neben dreizehn anderen Hallen vor über 120 Jahren gebaut und ist die beliebteste der wenigen noch existierenden. Jeden Freitag und Samstag versorgt man sich hier mit hochwertigen Lebensmitteln ausgewählter kleiner Händler. Unter der Woche wird bei Kochkursen, auf dem Breakfast Market, dem Naschmarkt oder dem Street Food Thursday gutes Essen zelebriert. Letzterer ist schon fast eine Institution geworden. Jeden Donnerstag kann probiert werden, was mit viel Fantasie von internationalen Köchen zubereitet wird. Angefangen bei Macaroni & Cheese, geräuchertem Fisch oder frisch gebratenem Schweinefleisch bis hin zu gesunden Versionen von Waffeln oder New York Cheesecake. Alles ist köstlich. Wer eine Pause vom Anstehen braucht, schnappt sich ein Bier – natürlich in der Region gebraut – und entspannt für ein paar Minuten in oder vor der Markthalle. Markthalle Neun is a farmer's market with a rich history, unique events, and a great selection of fair, organic, and local products. Built over 120 years ago, it is definitely the most popular among the few that are left. Come and admire the unique, clear structure of the building, the brick walls, the glass roof, and the well-incorporated wooden elements. Every Friday and Saturday, Berliners stock up on high-quality products sold by a select group of small merchants. During the rest of the week, the hall hosts events celebrating good food, including cooking classes, Breakfast Market, a sweets market, and Street Food Thursday. The latter is a huge hit bringing locals, visitors, young, and old alike to try international cuisine served by incredibly creative chefs. You might start with mac and cheese, smoked fish, or freshly roasted pork, and finish with a healthy version of waffles, apple crumble, or New York cheesecake. If you need a break, grab a pint of local beer and relax for a moment.

Text & photos: Marta Greber

Markthalle Neun
Eisenbahnstraße 42/43, 10997 Berlin-Kreuzberg
Market: Fri&Sat 10:00-18:00
Canteen: Mon-Sat 12:00-16:00
Street Food Thursday: Thu 17:00-22:00

Nicht ganz so hip, aber bodenständig gut: die Moabiter Arminius-Markthalle, in der Arminiusstraße 2-4. Tipp: Anemone, der griechische Stand mit Imbiss. Less hip, but also great for food shopping: Arminius Market Hall in Moabit at Arminiusstraße 2-4. Recommendation: the Greek vendor and eatery Anemone.

FRISCHE KRÄUTER AUF DEM MAYBACHUFER MARKT FRESH HERBS AT MAYBACHUFER MARKET

Seit über 17 Jahren gibt es diesen Stand am Maybachufer: In der warmen Jahreszeit, von Mai bis Oktober, bringen Giesela und Reinhard Zülz frische Kräuter aus ihrem Gartenbaubetrieb Zülz in Wustermark an der Havel direkt zum Kreuzberger Wochenmarkt. Geerntet wird frühestens am Vortag oder noch am selben Tag im Morgentau. Im ständigen Sortiment sind Petersilie, Dill und Frühlingszwiebeln. Je nach Erntezeit kommen auch Bärlauch, Bohnenkraut, Portulak oder essbare Brennnesseln hinzu. Im Spätsommer wird das Angebot um schmackhafte Kartoffeln, Rote Beete und Möhren erweitert. Aber man sollte sich beeilen: Der Stand der „Kräuterfrauen" ist mittlerweile auch bei Berliner Köchen sehr beliebt und die Ware nach wenigen Stunden bereits ausverkauft. Giesela and Reinhard Zülz have been selling homegrown herbs at Maybachufer Market for over 17 years, every Tuesday and Friday in the warmer months. The herbs are harvested either on the morning of, or one day prior to, the market and are brought from their garden operation in Wustermark an der Havel to Kreuzberg. In addition to regularly offering parsley, dill, or spring onions, you can buy hard-to-find herbs such as wild garlic, savory, purslane, edible nettle, and other varieties depending on harvest time. In late summer, the range expands including tasty potatoes, beetroot, and carrots. Make sure to go there early: the "herb women" have become very popular, especially among chefs in Berlin, so the herbs tend to sell out within the first few hours.

Text: Elena Podlubnaja / Photos: Tobias Faisst

Maybachufer Wochenmarkt
Between Kottbusser Damm and Schinkestraße, 12047 Berlin-Neukölln
Location of the stall: go past Kottbusserbrücke and Ankerklause and enter the market from the left, with the river to your right
Tue&Fri 11:00-18:30

Neben regionalen Wildkräutern lockt die Bio-Kräuterei Oberhavel mit essbaren Blüten. Halt macht sie unter anderem mittwochs und samstags am Karl-August-Platz in Charlottenburg. Regional wild herbs and edible flowers are sold by Bio-Kräuterei Oberhavel at the market on Karl-August-Platz in Charlottenburg on Wednesdays and Saturdays.

Wenn wir für die Vorbestellung bei Volksspeisung zu spät dran sind, gehen wir auch gerne ins Avan – dem Restaurant im Shop Oukan in der Kronenstraße 71 in Mitte.
When we forget to place our order with Volksspeisung on time, we like to go to Avan for lunch. It's the restaurant inside Oukan boutique at Kronenstraße 71 in Mitte.

DER LIEBENSWÜRDIGE LIEFERDIENST ZUM LUNCH THE ALWAYS LOVELY LUNCH DELIVERY SERVICE

Das Cee Cee-Büro ist bis 13 Uhr ein wundervoller Ort. Doch spätestens dann drängt sich diese eine Frage auf, hängt wie eine dunkle, schwere Wolke über unseren Schreibtischen, bis es einer nicht mehr aushält und fragt: „Was essen wir heute?". Dank Volker Eichenhofer gibt es darauf eine Antwort: Volksspeisung heißt der Lieferservice des Fotografen und passionierten Kochs, der es sich seit 2013 zur Aufgabe macht, Berlins Lunch-Angebot zu bereichern. Bestellt wird online aus einer wechselnden Wochenkarte - oft vegetarisch, immer lecker. Seine Kreationen sind anzusiedeln zwischen Contemporary Cuisine und Hausmannskost. Vor allem aber macht Volker alles in Eigenregie: den Einkauf in der Frühe, die Rezepte, Zubereitung und schließlich die Auslieferung. Mit seinem Fahrrad transportiert er bis zu 60 Portionen an verschiedene Arbeitsplätze und bringt uns nicht nur ein paar Mal pro Woche Haupt- und Nachspeise oder eine Salatbox vorbei, sondern immer auch etwas Büro-Gossip und ein verschmitztes Lächeln. The Cee Cee office is a great place to be, until around one o'clock. Shortly thereafter, one question sets in and hangs in the air like a heavy scent until someone can't hold back and dares to ask: "What's for lunch today?" Thanks to Volker Eichenhofer, there is now an easy answer to that. Since 2013, the photographer and passionate cook has made it his business to enhance Berlin's lunch scene. Orders are placed online by choosing from weekly menu - often vegetarian, always tasty. Volker's creations can best be described as a fusion of contemporary cuisine and plain fare. But what makes his service truly special, is the fact that it's a one-man show: from shopping for ingredients in the morning to creating recipes, cooking, and delivering up to 60 servings to different offices by bike. Not only does he bring us full meals and salads several times a week, but more importantly, they come with a shot of office gossip and always with a friendly smile.

Text: Sascha Bente / Photos: Volker Eichenhofer

Volksspeisung
Menu, orders, and catering requests through volksspeisung.de

DIE WUNDERBARE WELT VON THONE NEGRÓN THE WONDERFUL WORLD OF THONE NEGRÓN

Betritt man dieses Geschäft, ist der Trubel am Rosenthaler Platz ums Eck sofort vergessen. Die Wände sind in dezenten Farben gehalten, das sorgsam arrangierte Mobiliar und der mit Teppich ausgelegte Boden perfekt abgestimmt. Willkommen in der wunderbar designten Welt der Ettina Berriós-Negrón (siehe auch S.78), die hier einen stimmigen Ort für ihre Mode geschaffen hat. Kleidung von der Stange findet man nicht, stattdessen eine feine Auswahl an langen Kleidern und matt schimmernden Seidenblusen - schlicht, mit Rundhals oder adretten Krägen, in jedem Fall hochgeschlossen. Kleine Boleros und bodenlange Röcke können dazu kombiniert werden. Nicht unbedingt Mode für den Berliner Alltag, könnte man meinen, doch jedem einzelnen Teil wohnt die magische Kraft inne, einem ganzen Outfit eine angenehm erwachsene Eleganz zu verleihen. Und kommt der Moment im Leben, in dem man sich von Kopf bis Fuß als Frau von Welt zeigen möchte, ist man hier an der richtigen Adresse. Upon entering the store, you will quickly forget about the hectic Rosenthaler Platz around the corner. The walls are coated in subtle abyss green and the furniture is carefully arranged, matching the carpeted floor. Welcome to the beautifully designed wonder world of Ettina Berriós-Negrón (see also p. 78), who has created the perfect setting for her fashion creations. You won't find an overwhelming number of clothes on the rack here; instead, a fine selection represented by her long dresses along with various shimmering silk blouses. All of her designs are sophisticated, like her simple round neck tops with or without elegant collars. Boleros and floor-length skirts complete the selection. Not quite the average Berlin wardrobe, you might think. But rest assured, most pieces can easily be down-dressed for your busy city lifestyle while adding a touch of grown-up finesse to your outfit. However, there are those times when grandezza is required, and you'll be happy to find some Thone Negrón pieces in your closet.

Text: Nina Trippel

Thone Negrón
Linenstraße 71, 10119 Berlin-Mitte
Mon-Fri 12:00-19:00, Sat 11:00-18:00
thonenegron.com

LIVE & LEARN

ENDLOS SCHAUEN UND BETRACHTEN IST EINFACH IN BERLIN. ERKUNDEN UND MITMACHEN EBENFALLS. DANN WIRD DIE STADT ZUM BEKANNTEN UND BEWOHNER ZU FREUNDEN.

IN A CITY LIKE BERLIN THAT CONTINUES TO EVOLVE, IT'S EASY TO FEEL LIKE A STRANGER. DON'T BE. GET OUT AND START EXPLORING THE CITY YOU LOVE.

TÜRKISCH FÜR FEINSCHMECKER
TURKISH LESSONS FOR FOODIES

Liebe geht durch den Magen, sagt man. Sprachgefühl auch. Zumindest wenn es nach Deniz Julia Güngör geht. Unter dem Namen „Türkisch für Feinschmecker“ bietet sie Abendkurse und Wochenend-Workshops für verschiedene Niveaustufen an, bei denen Vokabeln nicht nur gepaukt, sondern auch gekostet werden. Kulinarisches und landeskundliches Wissen über die Türkei inklusive. Afiyet olsun - guten Appetit! As the German saying goes, the way to a man’s heart is through his stomach. Perhaps the way to learning Turkish is through the stomach, too. Deniz Julia Güngör offers “Turkish for Foodies,” an intensive language course where learning vocabulary means sampling the words as well. The evening classes and weekend workshops are offered for different levels. What a great way to discover Turkey, one of the most popular travel destinations for Germans. Afiyet olsun - enjoy your meal!

Text: Nina Trippel / Photos: Martin Mascheski

Türkisch für Feinschmecker
tuerkischfuerfeinschmecker.de

köfte

Deniz Julia Güngörs Empfehlung für moderne türkische Küche ist in der Pappelallee 15 in Prenzlauer Berg und heißt Osmans Töchter. Deniz Julia Güngör's tip for modern Turkish cuisine: Osmans Töchter (Osman's Daughters) at Pappelallee 15 in Prenzlauer Berg.

MUSIK + KLANG
DIY + SURVIVAL
Recycle
The Essential Guide
KRAUTROCK
ACROSS THE GREAT DIVIDE
ELECTRIC EDEN
BERLIN

DWELLING PORTABLY
WILDWOOD WISDOM
Ellsworth Jaeger
Recycle
The Essential Guide

Ein guter Ort, um das neuerworbene Fachwissen in gepflegten Unterhaltungen mit vorzüglichen Cocktails einzubringen: die Bar Marqués im Untergeschoss des gleichnamigen Restaurants in der Graefestraße 92 in Kreuzberg. A great place for in-depth conversation accompanied by sublime cocktails is Bar Marqués in the basement of the eponymous restaurant at Graefestraße 92 in Kreuzberg.

BÜCHER UND MAGAZINE ÜBER KULTUR, NATUR & EXOTIK

PRINTED MATTER ON CULTURE, NATURE & EXOTICA

Seit 2013 hat Kreuzberg einen Buchladen, der wirklich heraussticht: Zabriskie. Der Name verweist auf „Zabriskie Point", Michelangelo Antonionis legendären Film sowie den gleichnamigen Ort im Death Valley, wo einst Michel Foucault auf Acid die Zeit seines Lebens hatte. Was also darf man erwarten? Bücher der anderen Art! Inhaber Lorena und Jean-Marie haben ein Faible für Lesestoff über Natur, Rauschmittel, Kultur und Gegenkultur, Avantgarde und Exotik und dazu passend eine Selektion an Magazinen und Büchern abseits des Mainstreams. Ob Diskussionen über Drogensachverhalte oder Unterhaltungen über Utopien, mit Lesestoff von Zabriskie punktet man mit ungewöhnlichem Wissen auf der nächsten Party. Amongst Kreuzberg's bookshops, one stands out in particular: Zabriskie. After all, the store's namesake, Zabriskie Point, refers to Michelangelo Antonioni's famous counterculture film and the area where Michel Foucault first dropped acid. So, what can you expect? Books with a bite. Like its name implies, Zabriskie has a love for culture and counterculture, the avant-garde, and the exotic. The Owners, Lorena and Jean-Marie, carefully curate magazines and books, specializing in culture that flies below the mainstream radar – from drugs to outsider art. Paw through a few pages in their reading room or take a book home with you. Either way, you'll be the star of the conversation at the next party you go to.

Text: Lydia Willie / Photos: Ivo Gretener

Zabriskie Buchladen für Kultur & Natur
Manteuffelstraße 73, 10999 Berlin-Kreuzberg
Tue-Sat 12:00-20:00

DIE FERIENWOHNUNG MIT PERSÖNLICHEM REISEFÜHRER

A GUEST APARTMENT WITH A PERSONAL TRAVEL GUIDE

Falls beim nächsten Besuch von Freunden in den eigenen vier Wänden kein Schlafplatz mehr frei ist, gibt es eine Alternative: Das My Plus One Studio Berlin. In einer kleinen, hellen Einzimmerwohnung unweit des Hermannplatzes hat Clare Freeman ein temporäres Zuhause eingerichtet. Die Wohnung wurde mit einem eigens entworfenen Möbelkonzept ausgestattet, das auf der Verwertung alter Parkettböden und Kupferrohre basiert. Neben ausziehbaren Sitzmöbeln, die man zu einem Gästebett umfunktionieren kann, versteckt sich im Hängeschrank auch ein Fernseher. Das Badezimmer wurde aufwändig saniert und ist wie in einem schicken Hotel. Alles in allem ein stilsicheres und sympathisches Wohlfühlzuhause auf Zeit. Und das „Plus One" soll natürlich auch nicht unerwähnt bleiben: Bei jeder Buchung ist eine Tour mit persönlichem „Reiseführer" enthalten – so kann man den Kiez mit einem Local kennenlernen. Next time you have friends coming to Berlin looking for accommodations, you can recommend the My Plus One Studio Berlin: a stylish one-bedroom apartment in the heart of hip Neukölln, conveniently located near Hermannplatz. Clare Freeman, who owns the apartment, renovated the place entirely, and turned it into a chic home away from home. The interior concept features custom made furniture using plenty of salvaged wood and cool gimmicks: a TV hidden behind an old cupboard, a sophisticated light system, and pull-out seat cubes that convert into an extra bed. The overall look and feel is simple, airy, friendly, and perfectly clean. The bathroom is like that of a posh design hotel! And let's not forget about your "plus one," the added bonus: each booking includes a private city guide of your choice, where a like-minded local offers a one-of-a-kind tour. A different approach to Berlin than what your average tour company offers.

Text: Nina Trippel

My Plus One Studio – Berlin
myplusone.net

Für tiefere Einsichten und Einblicke in die Welt der Kunst und Architektur mit Locals empfiehlt sich eine geführte Tour mit Niche (nicheberlin.de).
The best way to discover Berlin's art and architecture: book a tour at Niche (nicheberlin.de).

CEE CEE'S GUEST: BLESS

Im Wedding, zwischen Bausünden und unter diskreter Beobachtung von Anwohnern, Arztbesuchern oder Hundezüchtern, liegt das Berliner Studio von BLESS: Ein multifunktionaler Arbeitsraum, ausgerüstet für Handarbeitsproduktionen bis hin zu raumgreifenderen Versuchsanordnungen sowie mehreren Büroarbeitsplätzen. Hier arbeitet Ines Kaag, die eine Hälfte von BLESS, mit ihrem Team. Desiree Heiss, die andere Hälfte des Duos, lebt und entwirft in einer vergleichbaren Situation in Paris. Aber die beiden sind „weder Berliner noch Pariser, denn BLESS ist für uns immer eine Europäerin gewesen". Hier wie da binden sie Profis und Amateure, Migranten, Schüler oder „Daheimgebliebene" ein und „genießen die Vielfalt der verschiedenen Kulturen und Generationen". So entstehen an zwei Orten Kleidungsstücke, textile Objekte oder Home-Accessoires – für jene, die Kategorien brauchen. In jedem Fall Dinge, die den Alltag infrage stellen, und das schon seit 1995. BLESS lässt sich nicht fotografieren, gewährt aber an anderer Stelle Einblick: Wenn Ines nicht gerade nach Karlsruhe pendelt, wo BLESS eine Professur für Produktdesign innehat, dann zum Beispiel in ihrer ehemaligen Wohnung, bei BLESS HOME BERLIN (s. S.32). Oder bei einer Stunde asiatischer Kampfkunst im Studio Aikido Ryu Berlin. In Wedding, between construction sins and the resident's discrete observations, people visiting the doctor's, and dog breeders you'll find the Berlin studio of BLESS: A multifunctional work space, laid out for handicraft production, tentative workshop arrangements, and several office workstations to organize the production and distribution. This is where Ines Kaag, one half of BLESS, works with her team. Desire Heiss, the duos' other half, lives and works in a comparable setup in Paris. But the two are "neither Berliner nor Parisians as BLESS has always been a European for us." In both cities, they work with migrants and locals such as senior citizens and "enjoy the diversity of different cultures and generations." For those who need categories – BLESS produces clothes, textile objects, and home accessories, since 1995. Overall, objects that question our everyday life. BLESS does not permit pictures to be taken but allows insights elsewhere: If Ines is not on her way to Karlsruhe, where BLESS holds a professorship in product design, you'll get her in her former apartment at BLESS HOME BERLIN (s. p. 32). Or during an hour of Asian martial art in the Aikido Ryu Berlin studio. →

bless-service.de

Ausgleich in der Natur findet BLESS am Werbellinsee. Am besten mit einem Räucherfischbrötchen vom Restaurant „Alte Fischerei" in 16244 Altenhof, Am See 2.
To escape the city, Ines likes to go to Lake Werbellinsee – preferably with a smoked fish bun from the restaurant Alte Fischerei at Am See 2, 16244 Altenhof.

BLESS EMPFIEHLT: AIKIDO
BLESS RECOMMENDS: AIKIDO

Parallel zur Initialzündung von BLESS haben wir 1995 in Berlin mit Aikido begonnen. Unser gemeinsamer Traum und Plan, nach dem Studium möglichst unverzüglich ein selbständiges und unabhängiges Lebens- und Arbeitskonzept zu entwickeln, beinhaltete die Idee, dass Aktionismus langfristig mit dem entsprechenden Ausgleich auf körperlicher, seelischer und geistiger Ebene begünstigt werden sollte. Aikido (1942 in Japan von Morihei Ueshiba begründet) ist eine defensive Kampfkunst, die in der Eigenschaft des Budo förderlich ist für Konzentration, Fitness, Geschmeidigkeit und soziale Kompetenz. Dojo ist der Ort, an dem Aikido geübt wird. Wir betreiben Aikido auf unseren Reisen, erfreuen uns an der Gastfreundschaft fremder Dojos und daran, dass Aikido ein non-verbales Kommunikationsmittel und somit eine perfekte Touristensportart ist. Auch in der Greifswalder Straße sind Besucher jederzeit willkommen, und das Dojo, unter der Leitung von Christian Goguet (5. Dan Aikikai), gehört zu den schönsten der Stadt. When we initially started BLESS in 1995, we also decided to take up Aikido in Berlin. After our studies, our mutual dream and plan was to develop an autonomous and independent live-work concept. We felt that being proactive in life was key to our long-term success in realizing and maintaining balance and harmony on the physical, mental, and spiritual level. Aikido (founded in Japan by Morihei Ueshiba in 1942) is a defensive martial art that is conducive in the realm of Budo for concentration, fitness, flexibility, and social skills. Dojo is the place where Aikido is practiced. We practice Aikido on our travels, enjoy the hospitality of other dojos, and appreciate the fact that Aikido is a non-verbal means of communication: thus a perfect sport for tourists. Headed by Christian Goguet (5th Dan Aikikai), the Greifswalder Straße dojo welcomes visitors at any time, and is among the most beautiful dojos in Berlin.

Text: BLESS / Photos: Benjamin Lindenkreuz

Aikido Ryu Berlin
Greifswalder Straße 29, 2nd backyard, 3rd floor, 10405 Berlin-Prenzlauer Berg
Participation requires email in advance: aikido@snafu.de

WILDKRÄUTERWANDERN MIT ELISABETH WESTPHAL
HUNTING FOR WILD HERBS WITH ELISABETH WESTPHAL

Die Brennnessel ist die Königin unter unseren heimischen Wildkräutern. Das „Wunderheilmittel" enthält sieben Mal mehr Vitamin C als eine Orange und war die eisenhaltigste Pflanze, die wir bei der Wildkräuterwanderung von Elisabeth Westphal probierten. Wer von den rund 15 Teilnehmern noch nicht gefrühstückt hatte, bediente sich ausgiebig am 16-gängigen „Wildkräuter-Menü". Direkt vom Waldboden in den Mund gingen in den drei Stunden blaue und weiße Veilchen, überraschend süße Lindenknospen, Waldmeister, das leckere Feldsalat-Substitut Scharbockskraut, die leichte Knoblauchsrauke und Altbekanntes wie Gänseblümchen und Kirschblüten. Während man selbst noch leicht ungläubig Pflanzen pflückte, die bis zu diesem Moment den Stempel „Unkraut" getragen hatten, klärte die Ernährungsberaterin über Heilkraft und Verarbeitung der Wildkräuter auf. So manchen Gang zum Supermarkt kann ich mir jetzt sparen. The stinging nettle is the queen of our native wild herbs. It contains seven times as much vitamin C as oranges, and the highest iron out of all the plants collected during our herbal walk with Elisabeth Westphal. Afterwards, all 15 participants tried the 16-course wild herb menu, which was highly appreciated, especially by those who had skipped breakfast that morning. Within three hours, fresh herbs and weeds that came directly from the forest floor went right into our mouths: blue and white violets, surprisingly sweet linden tree blossoms, woodruff, the delicious lamb's lettuce substitute lesser celandine, and well-known species such as daisies and cherry blossoms. While we were busy harvesting what we previously thought were useless weeds, Westphal explained the healing power of wild herbs as well as how to process them. Why go to the supermarket to buy spinach when you can use stinging nettle instead?

Text: Juli Reinecke / Photos: Juli Reinecke, Julia Michaelsen

Kräuterwanderungen (herb picking tour) with Elisabeth Westphal
To sign up, just send an email to: oekomarkt.kollwitzplatz@grueneliga.de

LESEN UNTERM GLASDACH IN DER VERSTECKTEN BIBLIOTHEK

READING UNDER THE SKYLIGHT IN A HIDDEN LIBRARY

Am Rosenthaler Platz würde man eine große Bücherei nicht vermuten. Aber genau gegenüber vom Weinbergspark versteckt sich die Bezirkszentralbibliothek Philipp-Schaeffer in einem Hinterhof. Für eine läppische Jahresgebühr gibt es hier Bücher, Magazine, CDs und DVDs zum Ausleihen. Im unteren Stock lädt der glasüberdachte Bereich mit gemütlichen Sitzgelegenheiten bei schlechtem Wetter zum Schmökern ein. Wunderbar ist auch die große Kinderabteilung.
You might not expect a full-fledged library at Rosenthaler Platz, but right across the street from Weinbergspark, hidden in a backyard, you'll find the Philipp-Schaeffer City Library. You can read and borrow any of the books, magazines, CDs, or DVDs found on all three floors. There's a big space with beanbags and a huge glass roof in the back area, making this the perfect quiet spot to hang out and read during cold weather. It's also a wonderful library to visit with kids.

Text: Sven Hausherr / Photos: Martin Mascheski

Bezirkszentralbibliothek Philipp-Schaeffer
Brunnenstraße 181, 10119 Berlin-Mitte
Mon-Fri 10:00-19:30, Sat 10:00-14:00

Für Spanischsprachige: Der Kreuzberger Buchladen Bartleby & Co. in der Boppstraße 2 betreibt eine Mini-Bibliothek im Hinterzimmer. There's a tiny library in the back of Kreuzberg-based Bartleby & Co., a bookstore dedicated to Spanish literature at Boppstraße 2.

PERFECT DAY

IMMER AUF DER SUCHE NACH DEM SCHÖNEN LEBEN. DABEI LIEGT ES SO NAHE UND HEISST UNS SCHON AN DER NÄCHSTEN ECKE WILLKOMMEN. WIR SAGEN: BIS BALD. THERE ARE MANY WAYS TO MAKE A GOOD DAY EVEN BETTER. SOMETIMES JUST VISITING LOVELY PLACES CAN DO THE TRICK. TAKE YOUR DAY UP A NOTCH BY STOPPING AT OUR TRIED-AND-TRUE SPOTS.

DER PERFEKTE WOCHENEND-BRUNCH THE PERFECT WEEKEND BRUNCH SPOT

Friedrichshain „reimt" sich auf billige Cocktails, Hostels und Klassenfahrt. Trotzdem gibt es mehr zu entdecken als Happy Hour-Hopping. Fernab vom Touristentrubel versteckt sich am Traveplatz das Aunt Benny – mit Rucola-Bagel und frischem Himbeer-Ingwer-Smoothie startet man hier in den Tag. Wer am Wochenende ab mittags vorbeischaut, bekommt mit etwas Glück zu seinen Austern auch einen Bloody Mary von Tony Galea serviert, dem Barchef der Schwester-Lokalität The Antlered Bunny gleich nebenan. Friedrichshain is all about cheap hostels, hookah bars, and school trips. Yet there is more to be discovered beyond happy hour hopping. Far from the hustle of Simon-Dach-Straße, you'll find Aunt Benny on Traveplatz. Start your weekend with bagels, fresh raspberry-ginger smoothies, and a view of the park. The sister-bar next door, The Antlered Bunny, opens at noon on weekends, and if you're lucky you may catch chef Tony Galea serving oysters and Bloody Marys.

Text: Laura Storfner / Photos: Hanna Skoog

Aunt Benny & The Antlered Bunny
Oderstraße 7, 10247 Berlin-Friedrichshain
Café: Tue-Fri 9:00-20:00, Sat&Sun 10:00-20:00
Bar: Tue-Fri 18:00-2:00, Sat&Sun 12:00-2:00
auntbenny.com

Auch gut zum wach werden und in den Friedrichshainer Morgen starten: Silo in der Gabriel-Max-Straße 4 hat den besten Kaffee im Viertel. Wake up Friedrichshain and smell the coffee! Silo at Gabriel-Max-Straße 4 serves the best brew in the neighborhood.

WILLLKOMMEN IM WUNDERLAND DER MAGAZINE WELCOME TO MAGAZINE WONDERLAND

Schönes und Schlaues am Puls der Zeit aus den Bereichen Design, Kunst und Mode. Von Hochglanz- und Special-Interest-Zeitschriften über Fanzines bis hin zu einer Auswahl an Büchern – all killer no filler. Selbst wenn ich meinen Shopping-Ausflug in Mitte kurzhalten will, bleibe ich am Ende doch immer mindestens eine Stunde in diesem Magazin-Store, an dem kein Weg vorbeiführt. The shop specializes in cutting-edge magazines – beautiful and smart stuff can be found on the shelves. Well-known magazines, literature, and self-published fanzines – all killer, no filler. Even if I want to keep my shopping excursion to Mitte as short as possible, in the end I'll spend an hour in do you read me?!. It's inevitable.

Text: Sascha Bente / Photos: Achim Hatzius

do you read me?!
Auguststraße 28, 10117 Berlin-Mitte
Mon-Sat 10:00-19:30

BROTZEIT IN MITTE WATCH ARTISAN BAKERS IN ACTION

Dieser Ableger einer Bio-Bäckerei aus Frankfurt am Main ist eine willkommene Bereicherung in Berlin. Hier kann man den Bäckern bei der Arbeit zusehen, denn die Backstube ist durch eine große Glasscheibe vom Laden und Café abgetrennt. Das Sortiment umfasst von Oliven-Ciabatta bis Vollkornbrot alles, was das Brotesserherz begehrt. Anständige Laugenbrezeln, Kuchen, Quiches oder belegte Brote gibt es auch, und die Zimtschnecken sind riesig, saftig, aromatisch, lecker – alleine dafür kommt man wieder! With the first Zeit für Brot in Frankfurt am Main, Berlin has become the organic bakery's second location. It is divided into two parts: shop/café and bakery behind the window – so you can watch the bakers in action. They offer a wide variety of baked goods, from white breads such as the olive ciabatta to heavy wholegrain loafs and everything in between. Fresh Laugenbrezel is also available as well as cakes, quiches, and more. The cinnamon roll – Zimtschnecke in German – is lovely, juicy, yummy, and definitely worth coming back for.

Text: Nina Trippel / Photos: Marta Greber

Zeit für Brot
Alte Schönhauser Straße 4, 10119 Berlin-Mitte
Mon-Fri 7:30-20:00, Sat 8:00-20:00, Sun 8:00-18:00, Holidays 8:00-16:00
zeitfuerbrot.com

Eine weitere „gläserne" Bäckerei ist Endorphina Backkunst in der Elsenstraße 52 in Neukölln. Der ideale Ort, um für das Picknick im Treptower Park einzukaufen. Endorphina Backkunst in Neukölln is another bakery where you can see the bakers at work. Located at Elsenstraße 52, it's the perfect place to stop before riding to Treptower Park for a picnic.

RUDERPARTIE AUF DEM STECHLINSEE ROW BOATING ON LAKE STECHLIN

Spätsommer. Maisfelder. Sonnenblumengesichter. Und wenn es in Brandenburg ein Hawaii gibt, dann ist es hier am Stechlinsee. Dieser ist nur von einem Ort mit dem Auto erreichbar, und zwar von Neuglobsow. Man spaziert durch den dichten Buchenwald, bis die türkisfarbene Wasseroberfläche durch die Bäume glitzert. Wir verbringen den ganzen Tag mit den Ruderbooten auf dem See, schwimmen, essen Kuchen und entdecken Sandbänke, Fische und Taucher. Das Wasser ist glasklar und verändert je nach Sonneneinstrahlung seine Farbe von Azur über Aquamarin bis hin zu Gewitterblau. Mit 70 Meter Tiefe und einer Unterwassersichtweite von bis zu sechs Metern ist er der klarste, tiefste und mit Sicherheit der schönste See bei Berlin. In the summertime, cornfields and sunflowers greet you before arriving at Lake Stechlin, the deepest lake in the Berlin area. This is probably the closest thing you'll find to Hawaii around here. If you're driving, the lake can be accessed through a town called Neuglobsow. In order to take a dip in the sparkling turquoise water however, you must first go through the lush beech forest. You can easily spend the whole day here doing leisure activities: chill in a rowboat, make friends with fish and divers, explore the shores, enjoy food and drinks, and of course swim. The water is crystal clear, its hue ranging from azure to aquamarine to pure blue. Lake Stechlin is by far the most beautiful lake in this area.

Text & photos: Milena Kalojanov

Stechlinsee
16775 Stechlin

Statt mit dem Auto aufs Land, mit der Tram 62 zum See: Sandige Buchten und flache Ufer warten am Habermannsee in Mahlsdorf. Instead of driving to the countryside, take tram 62 to a city lake: sandy beaches and shallow water await you at the Habermannsee in Mahlsdorf.

MR. MINSCHS KUCHENPARADIES
MR. MINSCH'S CAKE PARADISE

Fernab vom Kreuzberger Kieztreiben befindet sich die Kuchenoase von Andreas Minsch. Bestanden von großen und kleinen Pflanzen, Blumen und einem kleinen Brunnen, gibt ein großes Schaufenster Einblicke in die Backstube. Hier kann jeder dem Konditormeister und seinen Gesellen bei der Arbeit zusehen. Die Einrichtung des Ladenlokals ist mit den cremeweißen Fliesen und Gerätschaften bewusst im Stil der 1950er-Jahre gehalten. Den Kuchen sucht man sich am besten vorher in der Vitrine aus. Das Sortiment reicht von Kirsch-Vanille-Streusel über Zimtrollen, Gebäck und Plätzchen bis hin zu üppigen Sahnetorten. Sonntags ist die Auswahl riesig, der Andrang aber auch. Ein Stück Kuchen ist so groß, dass davon locker zwei Personen satt werden. Off the beaten path, at Yorckstraße 15, you'll find the cake oasis of Andreas Minsch. Surrounded by numerous plants and flowers and a little fountain, the huge windowpane lets you peep inside the bakery. Here you can watch the confectioner and his apprentices at work. The shop has a 1950s look to it and is decorated with cream white tiles. Choose from the various cakes on display in the case: cherry-vanilla crumble, cinnamon rolls, pastries, cookies, and sumptuous cream tarts. On Sundays the assortment is bigger but likewise is the number of customers. A piece of cake is so huge (and fantastic) it feeds two. Check out Mr. Minsch's Facebook page to get an idea of all the delicacies sold here - from chocolate artworks to multi-level wedding cakes.

Text: Nikolaus Hurlbrink / Photos: Marta Greber

Mr. Minsch
Yorckstraße 15, 10965 Berlin-Kreuzberg
Daily 10:00-22:00

DIE WUNDERBARE WELT DER SCHREIBWAREN THE LITTLE GREAT STATIONERY SHOP

Weil mir das Schreiben und Antworten per Post noch immer Spaß macht, kann ich jedem diese Papeterie ans Herz legen. Hier gibt es handgedruckte Einladungen und Grußkarten, meist in kleinen Auflagen, die mit Techniken wie Buch-, Siebdruck und Holzschnitt hergestellt werden. Die Entscheidung zwischen Notizheften, Kalendern, Brief- und Geschenkpapieren fällt nicht leicht, und wer noch nicht genug hat: Stifthalter, klammerlose Hefter, Scheren, Falzbeine, Blattwender und Heftnotizen ergänzen die Auswahl. In der Gewissheit, nicht die einzige Briefschreiberin zu sein: répondez s'il vous plaît!

I really enjoy writing letters and responding to them. Thus I can strongly recommend this stationary store where you'll find hand printed invites and cards - most of them using classic techniques, such as silkscreen or letterpress, in small editions, as well as classic writing utensils. Trying to make up your mind between the most beautiful notebooks, calendars, letter writing sets, and wrapping paper is not easy. And if that's not enough, there are steel rulers, bone folders, and stickies to choose from. I'd love to call them all my own. Knowing that I'm not the only letter writer out there: Répondez, s'il vous plaît!

Text: Milena Kalojanov / Photos: A. Kroth, Christine Davis

R.S.V.P. Papier in Mitte
Mulackstraße 14, 10119 Berlin-Mitte
Mon-Thu 12:00-19h, Fri-Sat 12:00-20:00
rsvp-berlin.de

LIEBENSWÜRDIGKEIT HAUSGEMACHT HOMEMADE LOVELINESS

Ein selbstgezimmerter Holztresen, Pflanzen, die von der Decke hängen und die Tische dekorieren - hier ist es unglaublich gemütlich und dezent amerikanisch. Durch die Vitrine mit Objekten wie z.B. einer alten Schreibmaschine verströmt das Roamers außerdem den Hauch einer vergangenen Ära. Der Befriedigung zeitgenössischer Bedürfnisse steht dies aber nicht im Wege: WLAN versorgt die technischen Geräte, Magazine Lesewillige und die kleine Tageskarte lässt keinen Wunsch offen. Ob Birchermüesli zum Frühstück, Shakshuka zum Lunch, gegrillte Sandwiches mit Ziegenkäse und Hummus für zwischendurch, Haferflocken-Orangen-Cookies am Nachmittag oder Smoothies zum Energie-Tanken: Alles ist hausgemacht und mit viel Liebe zubereitet. Ziemlich gut ist auch, dass jedes (!) Gericht mit Avocado ergänzt werden kann. Letztlich ist es aber die entspannte, einladende Atmosphäre, die das Roamers so sympathisch macht. Und natürlich die zwei äußerst liebenswürdigen Betreiber, Flore und Chris. Ich habe mein zweites Wohnzimmer gefunden. The timber counter and the little succulents hanging from the ceiling give this place a slightly American vibe. Eclectic objects are on display in the glass cabinet, including an old type writer that captures the flair of a bygone era. But rest assured, today's needs are met here, too: WiFi is available, magazines are waiting to be picked up, and the list on the chalkboard will tickle your taste buds. Start your day with a cup of great-tasting coffee or boost your energy with a freshly squeezed juice and some homemade Bircher muesli. Shakshuka, a grilled sandwich with goat cheese and dried tomatoes, or bread topped with sesame sprinkled avocado is perfect for lunch. What's also great: you can add avocado to any (!) dish. Everything is fresh and homemade, down to the hummus spread and the carrot cake in the bell jar. Besides the food, it's the truly lovely and attentive owners, Chris and Flore, that makes Roamers my favorite hangout.

Text: Nina Trippel / Photos: Sasha Kharchenko

Roamers
Pannierstraße 64, 12043 Berlin-Neukölln
Tue-Fri 9:00-19:00, Sat&Sun 9:00-20:00
roamersberlin.tumblr.com

Bei Gözleme in der Karl-Marx-Straße 35 in Neukölln schmeißen die Frauen den Laden – und bereiten die namensgebende türkische Spezialität zu. Women are in charge at Gözleme at Karl-Marx-Straße 35 in Neukölln. Atmosphere may be lacking, but their great tasting Turkish specialty is unbeatable.

64
Roamers
COFFEE & BOOZE
Roamers
COFFEE
SANDWICHES
POACHED EGGS
SOUP
CAKE
&MORE
come in

Ihren Sinn für schöne Produkte stellt Melanie dal Canton auch als Geschäftsführerin im Conceptstore von Andreas Murkudis in der Potsdamer Straße 81E in Tiergarten unter Beweis. Melanie dal Canton's sense of beautiful products can also be seen at Andreas Murkudis' concept store at Potsdamer Straße 81E in Tiergarten, where she is managing director.

EIN KLEINOD AUS KOSMETIKA
A PARADISE FOR BEAUTY FIENDS

Bei Truman Capote setzt sich Holly Golightly nach einer durchtanzten Nacht in ein Taxi zu Tiffany. In Berlin tut es ein Spaziergang zu MDC Cosmetic. Diamanten gibt es bei Melanie dal Canton nicht, stattdessen warten in ihrer Schatzkammer Perlen der Kosmetik. Die Mittagssonne taucht die schlicht gestaltete Boutique in ein warmes Licht – Strahlen fallen auf ApoManums Lippenbalsam, June Ainscoughs Haarbürsten, Öle von Susanne Kaufmann und allerlei Kosmetik von Aesop. Dazwischen findet man u.a. Kaschmir-Wärmflaschen und einen Handspiegel von Sarah Illenberger, der sich als Pingpongschläger tarnt. Körperbehandlungen, Maniküre und Pediküre werden ebenfalls angeboten. Ein Ort der Stille, an dem auch Holly ihre Augencreme gekauft hätte. After a terrible night, Holly Golightly would grab a cab and drive to Tiffany's – in Berlin you can simply walk to MDC Cosmetic. You won't find diamonds here, but cosmetic pearls in this treasure box. When Melanie dal Canton is not working for Andreas Murkudis' store, she's in and about her own empire. Rays of midday sun illuminate lip balms by ApoManum, June Ainscoughs' hair brushes, oils by Susanne Kaufmann, and countless products by Aesop. In between, you'll find hot water bags wrapped in cashmere and a cosmetic mirror masked as a ping-pong racket. Body treatments like massage or manicures are offered as well. A place of silence, where Holly would have bought an eye cream – and found a name for her hangover.

Text: Laura Storfner

MDC Cosmetic
Knaackstraße 26, 10405 Berlin-Prenzlauer Berg
Mon-Wed 10:00-19:00, Thu-Sat 10:00-20:00, Sat 9:00-20:00
mdc-cosmetic.com

DAS KLEINE SYMPATHISCHE ITALIENISCHE ESSZIMMER
THE CHARMING, TINY ITALIAN DINING ROOM

Familiär und gemütlich geht es im Sala da Mangiare, dem „Esszimmer" von Mauro Paglia zu. Das Menü ist übersichtlich, das Restaurant klein – aber genau das ist das Schöne daran. Antipasti wie gegrilltes Gemüse, Salat oder italienische Käse- und Aufschnittplatten stehen neben selbstgemachter Pasta auf der Karte. Alles wird frisch und mit viel Liebe zubereitet, Mauro legt gute Musik auf, und auch wenn es wie ein Klischee klingt: an einem der wenigen kleinen Tische fühlt man sich, mitten im Rollberg-Kiez, fast wie in Italien. Menu and venue are equally small at Sala da Mangiare, the "dining room" of Mauro Paglia, where both are just as nice. The short menu offers fine homemade food and the restaurant houses only few tables with a relaxed, familiar, and friendly atmosphere. Mauro is the chef, who prepares homemade pasta, antipasti, meat, and cheese starters, along with salads and desserts that accompany the wines and espresso. That's it. But that's what I love here: everything is simple. Altogether, a perfect place for a lovely, yummy dinner with your friends, surrounded by a touch of Italy in the midst of the Rollberg Kiez.

Text: Nina Trippel / Photos: Marta Greber

Sala da Mangiare
Mainzer Straße 23, 12053 Berlin-Neukölln
Tue-Sat 19:00-23:00
saladamangiare.de

Kennen sich und schätzen sich: Mauro und die Macher vom Caligari, dem fantastischen Italiener im benachbarten Schillerkiez, Kienitzer Straße 110. They know and appreciate each other: Mauro and the restaurateurs behind Caligari, the fantastic Italian restaurant in the Schillerkiez, just a few blocks away at Kienitzer Straße 110.

KUNST IN PRIVATEN GEMÄCHERN
ART COLLECTION IN A PRIVATE HOME

Nur wenige Sammler zeigen ihre Kunst der Öffentlichkeit. Die Sammlung Hoffmann tut dies und lädt zu einer Führung durch die private Bibliothek, das Kaminzimmer, den Flügelsaal und weitere Räume. Dabei trifft man auf Fotografien, Installationen, Malerei und Skulpturen von Künstlern wie Wolfgang Tillmans, Gerhard Richter und Frank Stella. Falls man der charismatischen Sammlerin Erika Hoffmann beim Flanieren durch ihre Wohnung persönlich begegnet, darf man auf Anekdoten über den Kunsterwerb hoffen. Very few collectors open their art collection to the public. The Hoffmann collection is one of them. You explore photographs, installations, paintings, or sculptures by artists such as Wolfgang Tillmans, Gerhard Richter, and Frank Stella. The very special thing about the tour through the collection – you pass through the private apartment of Erika Hoffmann: the library, the fireplace room, and the grand piano hall. If you're lucky, you might meet the charismatic collector strolling through her apartment enchanting her guests with a few anecdotes about how she acquired the artworks.

Text: Olga Schlosser / Photos: Lothar Schnepf

Sammlung Hoffmann
Sophie-Gips-Höfe, Entrance C, Sophienstraße 21, 10178 Berlin-Mitte
Sat 11:00–16:00; visits upon request and in the course of a guided tour
sammlung-hoffmann.de

Im Keller befindet sich der Projektraum FLEX: hier sind zeitgenössische Werke junger und etablierter Künstler im Dialog zu sehen. A project space is located in the basement: FLEX exhibits contemporary works by both up-and-coming and established artists and puts them in dialogue with one another.

DIE KULINARISCHE PERLE IM HINTERHOF A CULINARY TREASURE IN A BEAUTIFUL COURTYARD

Der Service in Berliner Restaurants ist normalerweise so schlecht, dass man fast erschrickt, wenn man plötzlich mit viel Aufmerksamkeit vom Personal durch den Abend begleitet wird. Im Katz Orange stimmt nicht nur der Service, sondern auch das Essen. Bei all den Köstlichkeiten fällt es allerdings schwer, eine Wahl zu treffen. So oder so: Auf jeden Fall Pommes Frites dazu bestellen – für mich die besten der Stadt. Und der Beaujolais ist famos! Die Küche, geführt vom ehemaligen Sous-Chef von Tim Raue, zaubert aus überwiegend regionalen Bioprodukten äußerst leckere Gerichte. Das im Hinterhof versteckte Gebäude hat etwas Magisches an sich und eignet sich für ein romantisches Dinner oder einen Abend mit Freunden. Except for very high-end restaurants, indifference and lacking are the words that come to mind when I think of restaurant service in Berlin. So when I was welcomed with so much attention and passion upon entering Katz Orange, it almost startled me. The restaurant possesses all the right qualities: great service, food, ambiance, and even price. The kitchen, led by Tim Raue's former sous chef, uses mostly regional organic produce to create its original delicacies. The beautiful building hidden in a courtyard is quite magical making it a perfect spot to bring a date or to dine and wine with a group of friends. By the way: the Beaujolais is fabulous and the French fries are the best in town.

Text: Sven Hausherr / Photos: Marta Greber

Katz Orange
Bergstraße 22, 10115 Berlin-Mitte
Mon-Sat from 18:00
katzorange.com

Regionale Bioprodukte zum Mitnehmen gibt es gleich um die Ecke bei Vom Einfachen das Gute in der Invalidenstraße 155 in Mitte. Local organic products to take home are just around the corner at Vom Einfachen das Gute at Invalidenstraße 155 in Mitte.

KALEIDOSCOPE

DIE STADT STRAHLT GRÜN IM SOMMER, IM WINTER TRÄGT SIE HIMMELGRAU. ABER SCHÖNE DINGE LEUCHTEN IN ALLEN NUANCEN. UND WOLLEN MIT NACH HAUSE KOMMEN.

BERLIN IS GREEN IN SUMMER AND GREY IN WINTER. BUT THESE PLACES ARE RAINBOW-COLORED ALL YEAR AROUND. TAKE SOME HOME WITH YOU.

DIE SCHÖNSTEN DINGE DER WELT THE WORLD'S MOST BEAUTIFUL THINGS

Hochwertige Produkte, oft von Hand oder in kleinen Manufakturen hergestellt, sind der Fokus des Süper Store, dem Geschäft von Vanessa Marangoni und Elisabeth Schotte im schönen Graefekiez. Hier findet man praktische Haushaltsutensilien wie klassische Küchentücher aus einer der letzten kleinen schweizerischen Webereien oder eine handliche Pfeffermühle aus Belgien. Auch im Angebot: Schmuckstücke von u.a. Christian Metzner aus Brandenburg oder edle Lederaccessoires von Il Bussetto. Der Süper Store ist und bleibt meine favorisierte Anlaufstelle für das besondere Geschenk und den Traum vom vollendeten Zuhause mit ausschließlich gut gemachten, echten und ehrlichen Produkten. Don't miss Süper Store when you visit the lovely Graefekiez. The owners Vanessa Marangoni and Elisabeth Schotte focus on carefully designed and crafted products and items for your home, including beautiful, handy household items like kitchen towels woven in Switzerland and a handy wooden pepper mill. Minimal yet eye-catching jewelry by Brandenburg-based Christian Metzner, leather purses and etuis by Il Bussetto roundoff the selection. Süper Store is the ideal place to shop for gifts or to get inspired and dream of your perfect future home furnished with only quality items!

Text: Nina Trippel / Photos: Florian Wenningkamp

Süper Store
Dieffenbachstraße 12, 10967 Berlin-Kreuzberg
Tue-Fri 11:00-19:00, Sat 11:00-16:00
sueper-store.de

Jede Nacht kann im Graefekiez enden: Bei einem Drink in der Minibar, in der Graefestraße 77.
After shopping: turn your evening into an endless night at the one and only Minibar at Graefestraße 77.

MAGIC
STIFF
ROPE
Kleine
Tricks
SPIONBRILLE
AVIATOR
POKER
SKAT
BICYCLE

SEIT
1884

EQUIPMENT FÜR MAGIER & MOTTO-PARTYS

ONE STOP SHOP FOR MAGIC SUPPLIES & THEME PARTIES

Zwischen Imbissen und Friedhofsmauern gelegen, könnte man dieses kleine, frei stehende Ladenlokal an der lauten Hermannstraße fast übersehen. Aber hineinschauen lohnt sich: Zauberkönig Berlin ist ein Traditionsgeschäft, das seit 1884 existiert und von Karen Goetzke und Kirsi Hinze seit 2012 neu bespielt wird. Innen erinnert das Geschäft noch ein wenig an die 1970er-Jahre – als Karens Opa den Laden führte. Das Sortiment bietet Klassiker und neue Gimmicks: Scherzartikel, Masken, Anklebebärte, eine kleine Auswahl an Kostümen und Accessoires für den großen Auftritt. Die ideale Anlaufstelle für Hobby-Magier, Motto-Partygänger sowie kleine und große Trickser. Located between low-key eateries and an entrance to a cemetery, this little store is easy to miss, but worth visiting. The shop Zauberkönig Berlin has actually been around for quite a while but since 2012 it's run by Karen Goetzke and Kirsi Hinze. The interior looks a bit like it did back in the good old days when Karen's grandfather ran the store. Zauberkönig stocks classic accessories for costume parties such as masks, and a few head to toe costumes. There are also gimmicks, gadgets, and all the essentials you need to launch a career as a magician. A perfect place for anyone looking for fun accessories or special gifts.

Text: Nina Trippel

Zauberkönig Berlin
Hermannstraße 84, 12051 Berlin-Neukölln
Tue-Sat 11:00-19:00
zauberkoenig-berlin.de

Wer hier nicht fündig wird, sollte circa fünf Stunden einplanen und bei Deko Behrendt in der Hauptstraße 18 in Schöneberg das komplette Sortiment begutachten. If you still can't find what you're looking for, plan on getting lost in Deko Behrendt's world of party decorations at Hauptstraße 18 in Schöneberg.

TRÖDEL, MÖBEL, KURIOSITÄTEN & KAFFEE UNIQUE VINTAGE SHOP WITH A LITTLE CAFÉ

In der Flughafenstraße reiht sich ein Trödelladen an den nächsten. Die meisten davon überfordern die Besucher mit unkontrolliertem Chaos, aber nicht so die Stube: Hier werden die ausgesuchten Stücke liebevoll arrangiert. Trotzdem lässt sich in jedem Winkel etwas entdecken. Ein überdimensionaler Globus wartet auf einen neuen Besitzer, ein Skelett mit Partyhut lugt aus der Ecke hervor und aufgetürmt dazwischen: ein schicker Schreibtisch aus Metall, eine Werkbank aus Holz oder ein Drehhocker im angesagten Industrie-Look. Praktisch für Unentschlossene: Das Café lädt bei Getränken zum Probewohnen mit dem Möbel in spe. Aber nicht zu lange zögern, denn sonst schmückt das Objekt der heutigen Begierde morgen schon ein anderes Heim. Countless secondhand and junk stores full of odds and ends line Flughafenstraße, but Stube is different. This little shop is packed with hand-picked gems, and still remains an authentic Neukölln spot. An oversized globe awaits a new owner; a skeleton crowned with a party hat peeks out from a corner; and piled up between them are a stylish metal swivel stool, an old wooden bench, a desk made of metal, and furniture and objects of all shapes and sizes. The little café invites you to try out what might be your future furnishings. But don't sit on it for too long – your object of desire might be snatched away to prettify someone else's home!

Text: Nina Trippel / Photos: Martin Mascheski

Stube
Flughafenstraße 24, 12053 Berlin-Neukölln
Mon-Sat 12:00-18:00

Auf der Flughafenstraße lässt sich noch mehr entdecken. Unsere favorisierte Raststätte nach dem Spaziergang bergauf: Lava, Hausnummer 46. There's a lot more to discover on this street. Our favorite rest stop after a stroll up the hill: Lava, a superb restaurant at Flughafenstraße 46.

CEE CEE'S GUEST: RUT SIGURÐARDÓTTIR

Für das Fotografie-Studium kam Rut Sigurðardóttir von Reykjavík nach Berlin und fand ein Zuhause in Schöneberg. Aus zwei Jahren wurden zehn. Vielleicht wegen der Flohmärkte, Picknicks im Park oder dem Umstand, dass man in Deutschland Sekt ohne speziellen Anlass trinkt. Vor allem aber weil „Leute beobachten hier niemals langweilig wird", wie die Isländerin sagt. Aber nicht nur die eigentümlichen Berliner hat sie im Blick, sondern auch ihr Gegenüber. Das kann ein Politiker, Schauspieler oder ein Model sein, denn Rut teilt ihre Zeit zwischen Porträtaufnahmen und Modeshootings für internationale Magazine auf. Letzteres ist ihre wahre Leidenschaft und lässt Raum für ihre poetische Handschrift. Wenn sie während eines Shootings einen Zweig vom Wegesrand pflückt, dann nicht, um das Set zu dekorieren, sondern um einem Bild ihre Signatur zu geben. Es wäre aber auch nicht überraschend, wenn sie sich den Halm wie Lucky Luke in den Mundwinkel klemmen würde. Lässigkeit mit einer Prise Eigensinn ist ihr natürlicher Wesenszug. Auch in Stilfragen. Kein Wunder, dass sie ein Geschäft empfiehlt, das Eigenwilligkeit am laufenden Meter verkauft: Fichu. Rut's photography studies brought her from Reykjavík to Berlin. Two years quickly turned into ten – maybe because of the flea markets, the picnics in the park, and the fact that Germans drink sparkling wines for no particular reason. But, above all, because "people watching will never get boring here," she says. Rut not only keeps an eye on the Berliners around her; she always focuses on the person in front of her. This may be a politician, an actor, or a model, since Rut divides her time between portrait shoots and fashion shoots for international magazines. The latter is her true passion and it gives leeway to express the poetic side of her. She just might pick up a twig from the wayside, not to use as a prop but to add her signature style in the pictures. Nobody would be surprised to see her with a piece of straw dangling from the mouth in the style of Lucky Luke. Her overall vibe is laid-back but there's something headstrong about her too, which explains her approach to her work. No wonder she recommends a store that sells a chill sense of cool by the meter: Fichu. →

rutsig.com

Direkt neben Fichu gibt es laut Rut den besten Kaffee Berlins, bei Double Eye. According to Rut, you'll find Berlin's best coffee at Double Eye right next to Fichu.

RUT SIGURÐARDÓTTIR EMPFIEHLT: FICHU

RUT SIGURÐARDÓTTIR RECOMMENDS: FICHU

Es ist eine kleine Herausforderung, sich den Weg durch die bunte Landschaft aus Vintage-Stoffen in diesem legendären Schöneberger Geschäft zu bahnen. Aber mit Oleg an der Seite – dem Herrn des Hauses – findet man nicht nur Schönes fürs Auge, sondern auch Futter für die Seele. Fichu ist ein auf Vintage-Stoffe spezialisierter Shop mit Meterware aus den 1920 bis 1960er-Jahren. Seit über 85 Jahren in Betrieb, ist der Laden nicht nur der letzte seiner Art in Berlin, sondern fast in ganz Europa. Und Oleg eine Szenegröße im Kiez – mit seinem langen Bart und der stilvollen Garderobe kann man ihn nicht übersehen. Ein Besuch bei Fichu ist eine kurze Zeitreise und ein Must für alle Vintage-Fans.

It's a challenge to make your way through the colorful maze of unique vintage fabrics in this legendary Schöneberg shop. But with the king of this castle Oleg at your side, you're in good hands. This place is a treat for the eyes and food for the soul. Fichu is a fabric shop that sells vintage fabrics from the 1920s to 1960s. Having been in business for 85 years, it is the last of its kind, being a one-of-a-kind shop not only in Berlin but in all of Europe... Oleg, the storeowner, has become somewhat of a legend in the neighborhood: he is undoubtedly a big part of its colorful characteristics. With his long beard, hat, and stylish wardrobe, it's hard not to notice him. A visit to this Berlin treasure is like taking a small trip back in time and is a must-do for all vintage lovers.

Text & photos: Rut Sigurðardóttir

Fichu
Akazienstraße 21, 10823 Berlin-Schöneberg
Mon, Wed, Thu, Fri 14:00-18:00, Tue 15:00-18:00, Sat 11:30-15:00

FLORALE AVANTGARDE & VINTAGE-OBJEKTE BEI MARSANO

AVANT-GARDE FLORAL DESIGN & VINTAGE OBJECTS

Blumen sind ein Stück abgeschnittener Sommer. Ein subtiles Arrangement in einer minimalistischen Wohnung. Wer jetzt zustimmend nickt und Marsano nicht kennt, der muss losgehen und diese Anlaufstelle floraler Avantgarde aufsuchen; er wird sich hier zuhause fühlen. Und dann nach Hause gehen – in der Hand, im Fahrradkorb oder auf dem Beifahrersitz ein in Papier eingeschlagenes Stück Dekadenz, duftend, blühend, prachtvoll. Allen, die ein etwas länger währendes Vergnügen oder eine „feste Bindung" suchen, sei Marsano Vintage ans Herz gelegt. Gleich nebenan findet man, ebenso stilsicher ausgesucht, Vintage-Objekte aus aller Welt. Flowers are a piece of summer and add the finishing touches to a minimalist apartment. Those who nod their heads in agreement, but haven't heard of Marsano yet, must head to this place – the go-to shop for avant-garde floral items. You will feel at home here. Take a part of the store with you: the fragrant, splendid, and blooming decadence will come gently wrapped in paper. Those who seek pleasures less fleeting can try their luck next door at Marsano Vintage. The shop features vintage objects from around the world that are just as stylish.

Text: Claudia Trippel

Marsano
Charlottenstraße 75, 10117 Berlin-Mitte
Mon-Fri 10:00-19:00, Sat 10:00-16:00
marsano-berlin.com

Mehr Galerie als Blumenladen: Brutto Gusto auf der Torstraße 175. Brutto Gusto at Torstraße 175 doesn't just sell floral art, but real artwork too.

Nicht für Bastler, sondern Pros: Modulor in der Prinzenstraße 85 in Kreuzberg – ohne dieses Geschäft ist Berlins Kreativszene unvorstellbar. Not only for DIYers: Modulor at Prinzenstr. 85 in Kreuzberg rocks the professional creatives' world.

DAS KUNTERBUNTE DO-IT-YOURSELF-UNIVERSUM
A PARADISE FOR DIY LOVERS

Mein Paradies heißt Hobbyshop Wilhelm Rüther. Das Familienunternehmen ist seit 1969 der Spezialist für Buntpapiere, Pinsel, Bienenwachs-Bastelsets, Farbpigmente, Dekopilze, Strohsterne und Kerzenhalter für den Adventskranz. Jeder Anlass eignet sich dazu, diesen Laden zu besuchen und sich zwischen all den Seidenpapieren, Styroporkugeln und Staffeleien zu verlieren. Geburtstage, Weihnachten, Fasching und Jubiläen – hier gibt es alles, was man zum Entwerfen und Basteln benötigt. Nach viel zu kurzen Stunden im Paradies fährt man mit seiner Beute und neuen Ideen nach Hause. Ohne diesen Laden ist meine Welt einfach undenkbar! Paradise has a new name: Hobbyshop Wilhelm Rüther. This shop has something for every occasion – for birthday parties, Christmas, carnivals, and anniversaries. It's easy to get lost between all the sequins, silk paper, Styrofoam balls, and easels. Since 1969, the family-owned business has been the one stop source for anything arts and crafts related: colored paper, brushes, silk ribbons, beeswax, craft kits, pigments, mushroom decor, straw stars, and candle holders ... After you've spent hours looking through everything and leave the shop, you'll be loaded with new treasures and bursting with ideas. This place rocks my world!

Text: Milena Kalojanov / Photos: Carlito Schilirò

Hobbyshop Wilhelm Rüther
Goltzstraße 37, 10781 Berlin-Schöneberg
Mon-Fri 10:00-19:00, Sat 10:00-16:00
hobbyshop.de

CEE CEE'S GUEST: CHRISTIAN SCHNEIDER

Auf ein Stück Kuchen am Nachmittag kann man sich mit Christian Schneider bestens verabreden. Am liebsten an einem unbekannten Ort, denn Neugier und Entdeckerlust sind sein Business. Zusammen mit Dirk Mönkemöller gibt Christian The Weekender heraus. Ein Magazin, das durch den entspannten, erwachsenen Blick auf die schönen Seiten des Lebens besticht. Wohnwelten und Orte für kleine Fluchten werden wunderbar bebildert und persönlich beschrieben. Jede Ausgabe will den Leser aufs Neue verführen, seinen Blick von den eigenen vier Wänden auf Anderes richten. Christian selbst ist gebürtiger Kölner und Wahl-Neuköllner und liebt es, Berlin mit dem Rad zu durchstreifen, „egal in welche Richtung". Dann schreibt er schon mal eine Nachricht und gibt durch: „Neue Nudelbar entdeckt – was für Cee Cee?". Wir folgen seinen Tipps, denn wir schätzen den Grafikdesigner-von-Beruf und Magazinmacher-aus-Leidenschaft auch als Mann von Welt. Eine ganz eigene Welt hat er auch Cee Cee vorgestellt: Die Heil Quelle. Und die hat, na klar, weniger mit Wellness zu tun, als mit innerstädtischem Entdeckertum. Having a piece of cake in the afternoon with Christian Schneider may be the perfect way to meet him. You should choose a place neither of you has been to, since his job is to discover the new and unknown: together with Dirk Mönkemöller, Christian publishes The Weekender. The magazine captivates readers with its relaxed, mature perspective on the beautiful side of life. It features stunning photos and interesting articles about unique living spaces and getaway spots. Every issue motivates its readers to engage with exciting new locations around the world. However, Christian, a native of Cologne and Neuköllner by choice, continues his scouting expeditions in Berlin, preferably by bike and "in whatever direction." Sometimes, we receive random text messages: "Discovered a new noodle bar, something for Cee Cee?" We trust his recommendations because we appreciate this graphic designer and magazine publisher as a man of the world. He has also introduced a world of its own to Cee Cee: the Heil Quelle ("healing spring") – a shop that's less about wellness and much more of an inner-city discovery. →

the-weekender.com

CHRISTIAN SCHNEIDER EMPFIEHLT: HEIL QUELLE

CHRISTIAN SCHNEIDER RECOMMENDS: HEIL QUELLE

Doris Heil betreibt seit Jahren einen Kiosk namens Heil Quelle auf der Pannierstraße und war eine der Ersten in Berlin, die den The Weekender ins Sortiment nahm. Vor einer Weile musste sie mit dem Laden umziehen und fand ein paar Häuser weiter einen Heimwerkerladen, den sie übernehmen konnte. Jetzt führt sie den wohl kuriosesten wie auch charmantesten Kiosk Neuköllns (wenn nicht ganz Berlins). Hier finden Besucher neben Pinseln, Packband und Sicherungen internationale Magazine und Tageszeitungen. Bier und Tabakwaren natürlich auch. Wenn Zeit ist, ist ein Pläuschchen mit der Chefin inklusive. Die ungewöhnliche Zeitschriftenauswahl sieht Doris Heil als Alleinstellungsmerkmal, schließlich sei das Angebot der Konkurrenz 0815, wie sie sagt. Und was bringt die Zukunft? „Weiterführung als Heimwerker-Späti beziehungsweise Schrauben-Tante-Emma", sagt Doris Heil und arbeitet munter weiter daran, zu einer Institution zu werden. For many years Doris Heil ran her kiosk Heil Quelle (which means "healing spring," a word play with her name) on Pannierstraße. This shop was among the first in Berlin to carry The Weekender. Some time ago she found a hardware store nearby and decided to take it over. Now Doris' has become the most curious and charming of all in Neukölln, if not the whole of Berlin. Next to brushes, packing tapes, and fuses, customers will also find international magazines and newspapers. You can chat with the boss if you have time, though beer or tobacco products will become obligatory in that case. Doris sees her unique selection of magazines as her selling point, since her competitors mostly sell "the usual junk." But what does the future hold? "I'll just continue as the handyman's kiosk/general supply corner store," says Doris, and happily goes back to transforming her second location into the institution that Heil Quelle has become over the years.

Text: Christian Schneider / Photos: Tobias Faisst

Heil Quelle
Pannierstraße 58, 12047 Berlin-Neukölln
Mon-Fri 8:00-20:00, Sat 9:00-20:00
heil-quelle-berlin.de

Für den besten Whiskey Sour geht es in die Weserstraße 42 – den mixen nämlich die Barkeeper im Tier, sagt Christian. Christian's additional recommendation: you can get the best Whiskey Sour at Weserstraße 42 – they are mixed by the barkeepers at Tier.

DER CONCEPT-STORE FÜR KIDS
A CONCEPT STORE FOR KIDS

Wer Kinder hat, hat wenig Zeit. Statt zeitsparend online zu shoppen kann man aber auch ein Erlebnis daraus machen: bei Tiny. In diesem Concept-Store möchte man selbst wieder Kind sein und all die coole Kinderkleidung anprobieren oder einfach nur in den Büchern versinken. Aber dann ist man doch lieber wieder erwachsen – mit dem eigenen Geldbeutel in der Tasche. Ich habe noch keine Kinder und bin trotzdem noch nie ohne eine kleine Tüte aus Anne Postrachs Laden gekommen. Wie soll das erst werden, wenn es soweit ist?

Having children means not having a lot of time. Ordering kid's stuff online is quick, but why not make an event out of it? Just head to Tiny the concept store for little ones by Anne Postrach. Located on Schröderstraße, this store is minimalist yet charming, offering lots of nice, "good" things. I wish I were little so I could wear all these amazing clothes and delve into the books. But then I'm lucky: I'm all grown-up with my own wallet in my bag. I don't have children, but I never leave this place without a small purchase in my hand. What will happen the day I have my own kids?

Text: Karolina Rosina / Photos: Philipp Langenheim & Corina Schadendorf

Tiny – Things for Kids
Schröderstraße 14, 10115 Berlin-Mitte
Mon-Fri 11:00-19:00, Sat 11:00-18:00
tinystore.de

Tiny things für die Großen? Filigranen Schmuck gibt es nebenan bei: Felicious. Tiny things for adults? Felicious stocks filigree jewelry right next door.

REISEN NACH FARBEN
TAKE OFF IN COLORS

Feride Uslu fällt auf. Mit ihren langen, rotbraunen Haaren, ihrem bunten Signature-Look und weißen, mit Stickern beklebten Auto, mit dem sie durch Berlin cruist. Uns hebt sie auch hervor: mit Airbrush-Make-up, Nagellacken und Lippenstiften. Mein Favorit war lange „HAJ" – benannt nach einem Flughafen, wie alle Produkte. In diesem Fall bekommen Hannover-Langenhagen und ich für dieses ganz speziell leuchtende, pinkstichige Rot jedes Mal Komplimente. Was kann man von einem Lippenstift mehr erwarten? Die beste Anlaufstelle, um uslu airlines-Produkte zu kaufen, sind die Galeries Lafayette in der Friedrichstraße.

Feride Uslu has a striking appearance. With her long hair, her colorful signature look, and her fast white car with lots of stickers all over, you can't miss her. Thanks to her, the founder of Berlin-based makeup brand uslu airlines, and her business partner Jan Mihm, we too can become more lively and colorful. Her line features airbrushed makeup, nail polish, and lipstick. My favorite has been "HAJ" for a long time, a shade from their collaboration series named after an airport – like all their products. Whenever I wear "Hannover Airport," I get tons of compliments. What more could you ask for from a lipstick? One of the best places to purchase uslu airlines in Berlin is Galeries Lafayette on Friedrichstraße.

Text: Ida Marie

uslu airlines
usluairlines.com

TEMPELHOFER FREIHEIT, NEUKÖLLN

SCHLESISCHE STRASSE / CUVRYSTRASSE, KREUZBERG

LANDWEHRKANAL, KREUZBERG / NEUKÖLLN

WARSCHAUER BRÜCKE, FRIEDRICHSHAIN

STRAUSSBERGER PLATZ, FRIEDRICHSHAIN

KOTTI, KREUZBERG

Adalbertstraße
UZBERG

NEW CLASSICS

FÜR ALTBERLINER SIND SIE JUNGE HÜPFER. FÜR ZUGEZOGENE SCHON INSTITUTIONEN UND IKONEN DER STADTLANDSCHAFT – DIE KLASSIKER VON MORGEN. THEY MAY NOT HAVE THE PEDIGREE OF A 100-YEAR-OLD INSTITUTION, BUT THESE NEW PLACES ARE SIMPLY ICONIC. TRUST US, THESE ARE THE FUTURE CLASSICS OF BERLIN.

KUNST & KULINARIK IN DER EHEMALIGEN JÜDISCHEN MÄDCHENSCHULE FINE ART & FOOD AT A FORMER JEWISH GIRLS' SCHOOL

In der ehemaligen jüdischen Mädchenschule sind seit 2012 Kunst und Kulinarik unter einem Dach vereint: In den einstigen Klassenzimmern, Korridoren sowie der Aula zeigt Initiator Michael Fuchs zeitgenössische Kunst und Werke der klassischen Moderne. Gerd Harry Lybke präsentiert, zusätzlich zu seiner Galerie Eigen+Art, internationale Künstler im Eigen+Art Lab. Camera Work bespielt neben den Charlottenburger Räumen die erste Etage mit Fotografie und hat auch das der ehemaligen Präsidentenfamilie gewidmete Museum The Kennedys hierher verlagert. Für den kulinarischen Teil sorgen die Grill Royal-Macher Stephan Landwehr und Boris Radczun mit dem Pauly Saal, wo man in vornehmem Ambiente deutsche Klassiker wie Ochsentafelspitz serviert bekommt. Paul Mogg und Oscar Melzer bespielen in ihrem Deli Mogg & Melzer mit Pastrami-Sandwiches oder Matzeknödel-Suppe die Räumlichkeiten am anderen Ende des Gebäudes. Before it opened in 2012, it took one year to transform the former Jewish Girls' School (Mädchenschule) in Mitte, a protected historical building, into a space for arts and food. Initiator Michael Fuchs shows contemporary art as well as modernist works. Gerd Harry Lybke of Eigen+Art installed his Eigen+Art Lab, Charlottenburg-based gallery Camera Work added photography to the space, and The Kennedys, a private museum in Berlin, contributed memorabilia from the former First Family. For foodies, there is Pauly Saal, fine dining offered by the owners of Grill Royal. Paul Mogg and Oscar Melzer offer deli-style food at Mogg & Melzer on the other side of the building.

Text: Nina Trippel / Photos: Stefan Korte, Steve Herud, Ailine Liefeld

Ehemalige Jüdische Mädchenschule
Auguststraße 11-13, 10117 Berlin-Mitte
Pauly Saal: Mon-Sat 12:00-15:00 & 18:00-3:00
Mogg & Melzer: Mon-Fri from 8:00, Sat-Sun from 10:00
Michael Fuchs Galerie: Tue-Fri 10:00-18:00, Sat 11:00-18:00
Museum The Kennedys: Tue-Sat 11:00-19:00
CWC: Tue-Sat 11:00-19:00
Eigen+Art Lab: Tue-Sat 11:00-18:00
maedchenschule.org

Wer den ganzen Tag in der Auguststraße verbringen will, schlendert weiter bis zum kleinen Park am Gipsdreieck. Einen Namen hat die Grünfläche nicht, dafür aber viele Sonnenplätze.
You can spend your whole day on Auguststraße. Take a break and hang out at the small park located where the street meets Gipsstraße to enjoy some sun.

DIE FOTOGRAFIE-INSTITUTION AM BAHNHOF ZOO PHOTOGRAPHY INSTITUTION BY THE ZOO

Anfang 2013 musste die Galerie C/O Berlin aus ihren Räumlichkeiten ausziehen – ein herber Verlust für Mittes Kunstszene, war das ehemalige Postfuhramtsgebäude aus dem Jahr 1881 doch ein Gegenpol zu den vielen „White Cubes" und ein ebenso außergewöhnlicher wie stimmungsvoller Ort für die facettenreichen Ausstellungen mit Werken von Nan Goldin bis Annie Leibovitz. Inzwischen hat die C/O Berlin einen neuen, nicht minder geschichtsträchtigen Ort gefunden und bespielt das zuvor leer stehende, nun umfangreich renovierte Amerika Haus. Früher Sitz des Kultur- und Informationszentrums der USA, kann der Westen endlich eine neue kulturelle Institution vorweisen. When C/O Berlin was forced to close its doors in early 2013, it was considered a major loss for Berlin's art scene. The old royal post office, built in 1881, proved to be an exceptional place to exhibit photographic artworks. Always easy to convert, it wasn't a white cube, but an atmospheric exhibition space with a rich history, offering room for exciting dialogues between the works of Nan Goldin or Annie Leibovitz. After extensive renovation measures, in Fall 2014, C/O Berlin reopened in the abandoned Amerika Haus. With the former US cultural and information center on Hardenbergstraße as its new home, West Berlin now has its own high-class attraction, one that helps reestablish this part of town as a cultural center.

Text: Mathis Neuhaus / Photo: Mila Hacke

C/O Berlin Foundation
Hardenbergstraße 22–24, 10623 Berlin-Charlottenburg
Daily 11–20h
co-berlin.org

Zum Bahnhof Zoo pilgern Fotografieliebhaber auch wegen der Newton Foundation und dem Museum für Fotografie in der Jebensstraße 2. More venues for photography aficionados are nearby: the Museum of Photography and the Helmut Newton Foundation are both located at Jebensstraße 2.

KAFFEE WIE ER SEIN MUSS
THAT PURE FRESH CUP OF COFFEE

Wer die The Barn Roastery betritt, stößt direkt auf die Baristas, verwickelt in Gespräche mit ihren Kunden. Meistens geht es natürlich um Kaffee. Das ist genau das, was Besitzer Ralf Rüller möchte: Nicht nur feinen Kaffee anbieten, sondern auch die Geschichten dahinter teilen. Kurz nach dem Erfolg mit seinem ersten „Baby" (The Barn Coffeeshop, Auguststraße 58) eröffnete Rüller 2012 seine eigene Rösterei. Inzwischen röstet er mit seiner wunderschön restaurierten Probat-Maschine von 1955 rund 500 kg Kaffee in der Woche. Die Bohnenauswahl erfolgt durch „Blind Cupping"; das interessante Ergebnis: Seine Sorten stammt immer aus biologischem Anbau (auch wenn nicht alle „zertifiziert" sind). Rüllers Leidenschaft für Kaffee ist mittlerweile so groß, dass er die Bauern persönlich besucht, per Handschlag grüßt und veranlasst, dass die Kaffeekirschen zum perfekten Zeitpunkt von Hand gepflückt werden.
Als Gegenleistung verspricht er, die Bohnen nie zu mischen, sie aber so zu rösten, dass jede Sorte ihren einzigartigen Geschmack entwickeln kann. Dafür zahlt Rüller zwar weitaus mehr als bei „Fair Trade", aber wir wissen alle, dass es das Geld wert ist. Wer montags vorbeischaut, kann während eines Kaffees vor Ort die Röstmaschine in Aktion sehen. Upon entering The Barn, you'll often find the baristas engaging in conversation with their customers on the topic of coffee. This is exactly what Ralf Rüller, the owner of The Barn, wants: not only offer great coffee but also share the story behind it. Although his initial concept of the original "baby" Barn in Mitte was based on offering high-quality baked goods, Rüller quickly found himself immersed in the world of coffee and started his own roastery in 2012. Now he roasts 500kg of coffee in his beautiful 1955 Probat roaster every week. He chooses his selection by blind cupping, with an interesting result: organic beans are unanimously selected. Rüller visits the farmers, shakes their hands, and asks them to handpick the coffee cherries at the perfect time. In return, he promises to never blend their beans, and to roast them properly so their unique character emerges. Prices higher than fair trade average are required for such service, but it's worth every penny! Visit The Barn Roastery on Mondays to enjoy your cup while watching their roaster in action.

Text: Rei Matsuoka / Photos: Marta Greber

The Barn Roastery
Schönhauser Allee 8, 10119 Berlin-Mitte
Mon 11:00-16:00, Tue-Thu 8:30-17:00, Fri 8:30-18:00, Sat&Sun 10:00-18:00
barn.bigcartel.com

Auch schon ein „New Classic“: das koreanische Restaurant YamYam Berlin auf der Alten Schönhauser Straße 6, gleich in der Nähe. A "new classic" for lunch: Korean restaurant YamYam Berlin at Alte Schönhauser Straße 6.

PROBAT
PROBAT

Falls ein Regeneinbruch den Badespaß beendet: Am Wochenende kann man im Treptower Hallentrödelmarkt gleich gegenüber Stunden verbringen. Rainy weekend? Just go to the flea market, which is also at the Arena. You can spend hours inside the Treptower Hallentrödelmarkt.

ZUR MORGENERFRISCHUNG AUFS BADESCHIFF SUMMER MORNING DIP AT BADESCHIFF

Das Badeschiff ist kein Geheimtipp, darüber müssen wir nicht streiten. Trotzdem hier ein kleiner Tipp: Fernab von Partys und Open Airs auf dem Arena-Gelände, dient es tagsüber tatsächlich – man mag es kaum glauben – als Schwimmbad und bietet früh morgens eine eindrucksvolle urbane Kulisse. Keine Rutsche, kein Sprungturm, kein Chichi. Perfekt für ein wenig Sport und Erfrischung vor der Arbeit. Badeschiff is by no means a secret in this city, we know. But it is still uniquely Berlin! Besides parties and open-air events in the Arena, Badeschiff actually is – believe it or not – a swimming pool. In the early morning, serious swimmers can enjoy a few laps amid impressive urban scenery. No water slides, no diving boards, no gimmicks; just sunshine if you're lucky. It's the perfect location for your morning exercise before work in the summer months.

Text: Max von Thadden / Photos: Sasha Kharchenko

Badeschiff at Arena Berlin
Eichenstraße 4, 12435 Berlin-Treptow
May-Sep: daily 8:00-24:00
arena-berlin.de/portfolio/badeschiff

NEW CLASSICS

Direkt nebenan, aber gänzlich gegensätzlich: Die vielfältige Sammlung von Thomas Olbricht, präsentiert als „Wunderkammer". Right next-door but based on opposite concept: me Collectors Room. Here German art collector Thomas Olbricht is showcasing his eclectic "cabinet of wonders."

ZEITGENÖSSISCHE KUNST IN DER EX-MARGARINEFABRIK

CONTEMPORARY ART IN A FORMER MARGARINE FACTORY

Gegründet in den 1990er-Jahren, als Berlin noch mehr Experimentierfeld war denn „etablierte Großstadt", haben sich die KW Institute for Contemporary Art zu einer Institution für zeitgenössische Kunst entwickelt. Ohne an eine eigene Sammlung gebunden zu sein, sind die KUNST-WERKE als Ausstellungshaus in der Lage, ein variantenreiches und hochklassiges Programm zwischen etablierten Positionen und Neuentdeckungen zu bieten. Im idyllischen Innenhof der KW ist außerdem in einem verglasten Pavillon des Künstlers Dan Graham das Café Bravo untergebracht. Ideal für eine Stärkung nach dem Kunstrundgang: das Clubsandwich.

Founded in the 1990s when Berlin was more of an adventure playground than established metropolis, KW Institute for Contemporary Art emerged as a top address for contemporary art. Not bound to a collection, KUNST-WERKE offers a diverse and high-class program that balances established artistic positions with new discoveries. KW's beautifully calming courtyard is also home to Café Bravo, which is housed in a glass pavilion designed by Dan Graham. This oasis welcomes you during tiring art or shopping tours through Mitte. The club sandwich, in particular, will cheer you up!

Text: Mathis Neuhaus / Photos: Uwe Walter, Fette Sans

KW Institute for Contemporary Art – KUNST-WERKE BERLIN e.V.
Auguststraße 69, 10117 Berlin-Mitte
Tue-Sun 12:00-22:00
kw-berlin.de

DAS KÜNSTLER-CAFÉ AM SAVIGNYPLATZ ART-INFUSED FLAIR AT SAVIGNYPLATZ

„‚Fare un giro' heißt auf Italienisch so viel wie um die Häuser ziehen. Wir machen unseren giro jetzt täglich, und zwar genau hier", erklärt Igor Paasch, ehemaliger Maître des Grill Royal und Besitzer der kleinen Kaffeebar zwischen Savigny- und Ernst-Reuter-Platz. Gemeinsam mit Werbefilmproduzent Ralf Weber bietet er hier nicht nur Kaffeevariationen aus eigener Röstung an, sondern auch vegetarische und vegane Snacks: von ofenfrischem Banana Bread bis zu Linsen-Kokos-Suppe. Igor selbst ist eigentlich Künstler – ein Blick auf seine jüngsten Arbeiten ist in der Bestellung inbegriffen. Aber nicht nur Kunststudenten aus der UdK kommen hierher zum Mittagessen, sondern auch die Charlottenburger Nachbarschaft. "'Fare un giro' means to go for a walk in Italian. We take a little walk everyday and this is where it leads us," says Igor Paasch, the former host of Grill Royal and owner of this small coffee bar. Along with Ralf Weber, they not only serve their own roast, but also offer vegan and vegetarian delicacies at Giro Coffee Bar. Igor himself is also known as an artist – you'll find his latest pieces on the walls. Some of the regulars here are art students from the nearby university, but they are not the only ones; a colorful mix of West Berliners stop by regularly.

Text: Laura Storfner / Photos: Sasha Kharchenko, Loris Haller

Giro Coffee Bar
Knesebeckstraße 5, 10623 Berlin-Charlottenburg
Mon-Fri 8:00-20:00, Sat 10:00-18:00
girocoffeebar.de

ZEITGEIST IM KREUZBERGER HINTERHOF ZEITGEIST IN A KREUZBERG COURTYARD

Bis 2010 war die Oranienstraße eine eingesessene, alternative Wunderwelt aus Künstlercafés, Kultkneipen und Punk-Clubs. Dann kam Voo und der Zeitgeist. In dem Hinterhof-Concept-Store von Yasin Müjdeci findet man seither internationale Zeitschriften und Berliner Selfmade-Publikationen, britische Schraubenzieher und japanische Stifte, vor allem aber smart ausgewählte Mode. Viel Skandinavisches ist dabei: Carin Wester, Common Sweden und die größte Auswahl von Acne Studios der Stadt. Auch Design aus Berlin hat einen festen Platz, z.B. Mode von Hien Le und Reality Studio sowie Schmuck von Ina Beissner. Aber wo etwas herkommt, ist eigentlich nicht wirklich wichtig – man selbst kommt in den Voo Store, weil man weiß, dass man hier immer fündig wird – für sich und für andere. Eigentlich will man alles haben, was Einkäufer und Creative Director Herbert Hofmann hier zusammenträgt. Wen die Wahl quält, der nimmt am Holztisch Platz und bestellt beim integrierten Companion Coffee einen Iced Cappuccino. Aber selbst wenn man nichts kauft fühlt man sich danach bereichert, denn man weiß, was state-of-the-art ist. Until 2010, Oranienstraße was an alternative wonderland lined with artist cafés, cult bars, punk clubs, and a flower store that's always open. Then Voo Store by Yasin Müjdeci came – and the zeitgeist. The backhouse concept store carries international fashion magazines and self-made Berlin publications, British screwdrivers, and Japanese pens. But most of all: a smart fashion selection. Lots of Scandinavian labels like Carin Wester and Common Sweden, to name a few, and Acne Studios' biggest selection in Berlin. Berlin labels can be found on the racks too: Hien Le, Reality Studio, and jewelry by Ina Beissner. But do the origins of design really matter? No. You come to Voo Store because you know you'll discover cool items for yourself, friends, or your loved ones. But I must warn you: you'll want to have everything that the buyer and creative director Herbert Hofmann unites here. If you can't make up your mind, take a seat at the in-store café Companion Coffee, enjoy an excellent flat white or an iced cappuccino, and ponder. And if you end up buying nothing, at least you'll take some inspiration home with you.

Text: Nina Trippel

Voo Store
Oranienstraße 24, 10999 Berlin-Kreuzberg
Mon-Sat 11:00-20:00
vooberlin.com

STORE
Monday-
Saturday
11am-8pm
VooStore.

Zum Mittagessen kann man ums Eck bei Mundvoll in der Waldemarstraße 48 vorbeischauen. Nur mit Reservierung zu empfehlen: Milchmasthähnchen in der Henne am Leuschnerdamm 25. For lunch, check out Mundvoll around the corner at Waldemarstraße 48 or reserve a table and try the famous roasted chicken at the classic Berlin restaurant Henne at Leuschnerdamm 25.

Raus aus dem Bunker, rein in den Keller: Bei Sabzi in der Luisenstraße 15 speist man orientalisch und gesund – in Gesellschaft von Ärzten der benachbarten Charité.

Leave the bunker around noon and head to the subterranean eatery: Sabzi offers yummy Middle Eastern lunches. Your lunch companions are mostly doctors from nearby Charité Hospital.

KUNSTFÜHRUNG DURCH DEN BUNKER ART TOUR IN A FORMER BUNKER

Ai Weiwei hat hier einen sechs Meter hohen Baum aus Sumpfholz aufgestellt und dank Michael Sailstorfer duftet ein ganzes Stockwerk nach Popcorn. Christian und Karen Boros zeigen auf fünf Etagen die Highlights ihrer Privatsammlung und stellen damit so manchen Museumsbestand in den Schatten. Im Jahr 1941 als Luftschutzraum erbaut, wurde der Bunker in der DDR als Bananenspeicher genutzt und galt Mitte der 90er-Jahre als härtester Technoclub der Welt. Heute geht es hier ruhiger, aber nicht weniger aufregend zu. Ai Weiwei has set up a six meter tall bog tree, and thanks to Michael Sailstorfer, an entire floor smells of popcorn. This is no funfair, it is the Boros Collection – a five-story bunker bursting with a contemporary art collection privately owned by Christian and Karin Boros; they manage to dwarf some museums in size. The bunker was erected as an air raid shelter in 1941. It served as a storage facility for bananas in the GDR era, and its claim to fame in the 90s was housing the world's freakiest techno club. Nowadays, this place has certainly become more quiet, though no less exciting.

Text: Laura Storfner / Photos: Noshe

Sammlung Boros
Reinhardtstraße 20, 10117 Berlin-Mitte
Guided tours: Thu-Sun, must be booked in advance online
sammlung-boros.de

NIGHTFALL

FRÜHER WAREN KREUZBERGER NÄCHTE LANG. HEUTE PILGERT MAN IM MORGENLICHT NACH FRIEDRICHSHAIN. WER DAS DUNKLE SUCHT, FINDET ES ZU JEDER ZEIT. DAS LEUCHTENDE AUCH.

IT'S TRUE, BERLIN NEVER SLEEPS. EVEN IN THOSE WEE HOURS, THIS CITY NEVER CEASES TO AMUSE. NIGHTLIFE IN BERLIN CAN BE WILD, ENTERTAINING OR REFINED – THE CHOICE IS YOURS.

KUNST IM KINO ART AT THE CINEMA

Licht aus, Vorhang auf für: Videoart at Midnight. Einmal im Monat, immer freitags um Punkt Mitternacht, laden Galerist Olaf Stüber und Sammler Ivo Wessel zum cineastischen Rendezvous ins Kino Babylon. Videokunst von internationalen Filmemachern wie Douglas Gordon, Hito Steyerl oder Armin Linke findet hier ihren Weg auf die Kinoleinwand. Die Präsentationen hinterfragen dabei nicht nur filmische Inhalte, sondern auch das Medium selbst: Grenzen zwischen Kunstwerk, Film und Video werden aufgehoben. Lights off, curtains raised, spotlights on: Videoart at Midnight. Once a month on Fridays at midnight, gallery owner Olaf Stüber and collector Ivo Wessel invite you to a cinematic rendezvous at Babylon Mitte. They present video art by filmmakers and artists such as Douglas Gordon, Hito Steyerl, and Armin Linke. The presentations not only question content but also the medium itself. Art, film, and video become one.

Text: Laura Storfner / Photos: Jan Nicolas Harting, Knut Klaßen

Videoart at Midnight at Babylon Mitte
Rosa-Luxemburg-Straße 30, 10178 Berlin-Mitte
Once a month Fridays, 24:00; free of charge
videoart-at-midnight.com

Auch gut um Mitternacht: die Bar 3 in der Weydingerstraße 20. Hier trifft man auch viele Künstler. Another fun option after midnight: Bar 3 at Weydingerstraße 20, where artists of all genres like to hang out.

ENTSPANNT DURCH DIE NACHT IN DER BAR NAMENS LARRY

PERFECTLY IMPERFECT – A NIGHT AT A BAR CALLED LARRY

Von der Perfektion der durchgestylten Mitte-Bars waren wir ein wenig gelangweilt - bis wir eines Abends bei Larry hereinschneiten. Hier fanden wir genau das, was wir gesucht hatten: Einen rohen Raum, an dem gerade genug gemacht worden war, um ihn als Bar zu nutzen. Im Larry passt alles auf unangestrengte Weise zusammen: das nette Personal - ehemalige Pauly Bar-Barmänner - das Interieur, eine gute Soundanlage, die DJs, die Tanzfläche. Wir kommen wieder.

Circa 2013, we were almost bored by the perfection of Mitte's bars. But then we came across Larry. Here we found exactly what we had been looking for: great atmosphere and the finest drinks in a raw space. Renovated just enough to function as a bar, everything seems to effortlessly fall into place. The lovely crew - former bartenders from Pauly Bar - serves the drinks. The simple interior is equipped with a good sound system and a DJ team works the small crowd on the dance floor. It's my kind of place!

Text: Sven Hausherr / Photos: Sasha Kharchenko

Larry
Chausseestraße 131, 10115 Berlin-Mitte
Fri&Sat 21:00 until late

Viel gediegener, ohne Dancefloor, aber mit guten Drinks: das Melody Nelson in der Novalisstraße 2. No dance floor, but more dignified and great drinks: Melody Nelson Bar at Novalisstraße 2.

VOM MORGENKAFFEE BIS ZUM APÉRO IN DER LINIENSTRASSE

FROM MORNING COFFEE TO SUNSET DRINKS

Unweit der lärmenden Torstraße versteckt sich dieses kleine Café hinter Ranken von Wildem Wein. Von einem der begehrten Außenplätze kann man dem Treiben am Alten Garnisonfriedhof zusehen und köstlichen Kaffee trinken sowie hausgemachte Quiches und Kuchen essen. Hat man dann noch nicht genug, bleibt man einfach für einen Sundowner an der schönen Ecke sitzen. Dazu eine Schale salzige Mandeln, die der Vater des Besitzers nach eigenem Rezept selbst röstet. So bleiben die Berliner Nächte lang! When it comes to cafés on a sunny day, café Lois is my first choice. Off of noisy Torstraße, in a quiet corner, you'll find the café nestled snugly in a grape ivy-covered building. If you're lucky enough to find a spot outside, you can bask in the sun all day long, drinking one of the finest coffees in town, while people watching in front of the old Garrison Cemetery. The menu offers fresh croissants, delicious homemade quiches, cakes, and panini. If you're still not ready to leave when the sun starts to set, just stay. Order an aperitif and a bowl of salted almonds, hand-roasted according to the owner's dad's secret recipe, and enjoy the evening twilight on Liniestraße - a perfect start to a long night.

Text: Milena Kalojanov / Photos: Carlito Schilirò

Lois
Linienstraße 60, 10119 Berlin-Mitte
Mon-Fri 8:00 until late, Sat&Sun 9:00 until late

CEE CEE'S GUEST: HENRIK MAULER

Was kann nur die Torstraße, die unumgängliche? „Stilbildend sein, ohne gut auszusehen. Madonna, George Clooney, die Junge Welt und Obdachlose in trauter Einsamkeit nebeneinander her existieren lassen", sagt Henrik Mauler. Und genau hier, hinter einer biederen Fassade, lauern Utopien visueller Art – bei Zeitguised. Gegründet wurde das Studio für zeitgenössische Kunst an der Schnittstelle zwischen digitaler Abstraktion und Realismus im Jahr 2001 von Henrik Mauler und Jamie Raap. Mit bis zu zehn Mitarbeitern erschaffen die beiden in einer ehemaligen Gynäkologiepraxis nie zuvor gesehene, einzigartig animierte 3D-Bildwelten. Als freie künstlerische Werke, die in Museen weltweit gezeigt werden oder als Auftragsarbeiten für Kunden. Warum in Berlin? „Wegen der Ansammlung junger, enthusiastischer und kluger Talente und der Tatsache, dass es hier entspannter zugeht als auf vergleichbaren Pflastern." Abwechslung von den virtuellen Sphären findet Henrik bei ganz Realem und Sinnlichem: Essen. Wo er gerne am Abend vorbeischaut: bei Volta in Wedding. What is it about Torstraße? Henrik Mauler claims that this street is stylish without being beautiful – international superstars such as Madonna and George Clooney coexist in cozy solitude with the "Junge Welt" and the homeless. Behind one of the street's banal façades, visual utopias are in the making at Zeitguised. Henrik Mauler and Jamie Raap founded the studio for contemporary art at the intersection of digital abstraction and realism in 2001. In a former gynecology clinic, a team of artists and up to ten assistants create the world of unique 3D animation. Their works range from independent art projects displayed in museums around the world to commissioned deals by international clients. Why in Berlin? "Because of its concentration of young, enthusiastic, clever talent and the fact that the scene here is more relaxed than in comparable cities," says Henrik. When he needs a change of scenery, he exits the virtual sphere and heads for something real and sensual: food. Where he likes to dine? At Volta in Wedding. →

zeitguised.com

Mittags trifft man Henrik oft in der Rosa-Luxemburg-Straße 7 bei Dolores in Mitte, weil er gerne scharf und glutenfrei isst. You can often spot Henrik having lunch at Dolores at Rosa-Luxemburg-Straße 7 in Mitte.

HENRIK MAULER EMPFIEHLT: DAS RESTAURANT VOLTA

HENRIK MAULER RECOMMENDS: RESTAURANT VOLTA

Von der Torstraße kommend, gefühlt schon tief im Wedding, stößt man auf einen flachen Pavillon, eine Art Béton brut-Raumstation mit Satellitenschüssel-Fassade. Hier sind Moustaches und Fixies noch homöopathisch dosiert. Innen empfängt einen die Berliner Schule: minimalistisch, unaufgeregt und stilsicher, mit cleanen Oberflächen, ohne alt zu wirken. Der Raum ist perfekt proportioniert, die Abendbeleuchtung on the spot, und den wenigen Dampf, den die offene Küche in den Raum entlässt, übersetzt der Gaumen sofort in eine Bestellaufforderung. Etwaiger Widerstand wird kurzgeschlossen – mit dem im Wedding gebrauten Eschenbräu. Die Freundlichkeit der Gastgeber ist auf gleichem Niveau wie der saftige "Volta Burger", dessen Fleisch, BBQ-Sauce und Sweet-Dough-Bun das Feld der Berliner Burgerliga von hinten aufrollt. Die Fries werden à la Julienne serviert und sind damit komplett crunchy: instant addiction! Ein anständiges Gespräch kann erst aufkommen, wenn die Tüte leer ist. Das Volta ist in jeder Hinsicht erfreulich zeitgemäß – wer glaubt, ungezwungenes Pub-Feeling sei unvereinbar mit gutem Essen und dem "Cool Berlin"-Stil, wird hier auf freundlich-lockere Art eines Besseren belehrt. Coming from Torstraße and finding the flat pavilion in a béton brut space station with a satellite dish façade, you know you're in Wedding. Mustaches and fixies are still found in homeopathic doses here. The interior style is Berlin school: minimal, calm, and stylish. Many surfaces are left bare, without appearing old. The room is perfectly proportioned, the evening lighting spot on, and the little steam released from the open kitchen is immediately translated by the palate into a request to order. Possible resistance is short-circuited with the Eschenbräu brewed in Wedding. The friendliness of the hosts is on the same level as Volta's juicy burger: meat, BBQ sauce, and sweet buns are at the top of the Berlin burger league. The fries are julienned and therefore entirely crunchy, an instant addiction; a decent conversation can begin only after the bag has been emptied. Volta feels stunningly contemporary in all respects. If you think a casual London pub feel is incompatible with exceptional food and the "cool Berlin" style, you will be taught a lesson in a friendly, convincing way.

Text: Henrik Mauler / Photos: Marta Greber

Volta
Brunnenstraße 73, 13355 Berlin-Wedding
Tue-Sun 18:00 until late
dasvolta.com

Veggie-Herzen schlagen auch in Mitte höher: verführerische Haute Cuisine gibt es im Cookies Cream in der Behrenstraße 55. Vegetarians have another reason to be thrilled: the chic restaurant Cookies Cream at Behrenstraße 55 in Mitte offers refined cuisine.

VEGETARISCHES DINNER IM EHEMALIGEN STADTBAD

VEGETARIAN DINNER IN A FORMER POOL

Abreißzettel in der Stadt verkünden: In der Gerichtstraße ist ein Riesenperlhuhn entlaufen! Wer es aufspürt, bringt es am besten zurück in die Stattbar – zu seinen Besitzern Sylvio und Maik. Der Finderlohn wird dort immer dienstags in Naturalien ausgezahlt: als vegetarisches Drei-Gänge-Menü. Wer keine Hinweise geben kann, ist trotzdem zur Dinner-Reihe "Lost in Wedding" eingeladen. Wechselnde Küchenteams zaubern für Stammgäste aus der Nachbarschaft und alle, die es werden wollen, Gerichte aus vorwiegend lokalen, saisonalen Zutaten. Zum Beispiel: Kohlrabi-Carpaccio mit Kapern-Dressing gefolgt von Ravioli mit Pilzfüllung. Und zum Dessert: Schoko-Brownie mit Ananasragout und salziger Karamellsoße. Die Speisekarte wird vorab online und auf Facebook veröffentlicht. Perlhühner kommen nicht auf den Teller – versprochen! A giant bird – a guinea fowl – just escaped from Gerichtstraße. Whoever finds it is advised to return it to Stattbar owners Sylvio and Maik. You will be generously rewarded. The payment is something yummy and is only awarded on Tuesday evenings in the form of a vegetarian three-course dinner. If you wish to attend without the lost bird, you may simply join the dinner series "Lost in Wedding" as a guest, too. The kitchen staff changes but the concept remains the same. All dishes are made from local, seasonal, and international ingredients. How does turnip cabbage carpaccio with caper dressing, followed by ravioli stuffed with wild mushrooms, and warm brownies drizzled with pineapple and salty caramel sauce sound? The menu is published online on Facebook in advance.

Text: Laura Storfner / Photos: Anna-Maria Scharf, Jan Kapitän

Lost in Wedding
Stattbar at Stattbad, Gerichtstraße 65, 13347 Berlin-Wedding
Tue from 19:00, reservations: stattbar@stattbad.net
stattbad.net

FEINSTER GIN IN ALL SEINEN FACETTEN GIN COCKTAILS FOR DISCERNING PATRONS

Die Berliner Gastro-Szene spezialisiert sich immer mehr. Ein Beispiel hierfür ist das G&T in Mitte, eine mondäne Gentlemen-Bar aus vergangenen Zeiten, ohne Chichi und aufs Wesentliche konzentriert: den Alkohol. Hier wird, wie könnte es auch anders sein, unglaublich guter Gin Tonic ausgeschenkt. Unter den vielen Gin-Sorten sind einige Raritäten. Hier startet man in die Nacht oder verbringt den ganzen Abend am Tresen, um diesen Wacholderschnapps – als Klassiker oder Neukreation – in all seinen Facetten zu genießen. These days the bar and restaurant scene in Berlin is becoming increasingly specialized. One of the recent additions is the G&T Bar in Mitte. A bar like this was definitely lacking in this neighborhood. Reminiscent of an old world gentleman's club, this bar is no meat market. What they offer here is what matters most: quality liquor and, to no surprise, an incredibly wide selection of gin and tonic drinks. The G&T Bar boasts an extensive collection of different gins, and only gins, most of which I'd never heard of. A perfect bar to start the evening with close friends or to stay all night enjoying this widely popular and extremely versatile juniper berry infused spirit in classic or new cocktails.

Text: Sven Hausherr / Photos: Katja Hendlmayr

G&T Bar
Friedrichstraße 113, 10117 Berlin-Mitte
Mon-Sun 20:00-3:00

Weinliebhaber schauen bei Maxim in der Gormannstraße 25 vorbei. Zu einem Glas Naturwein bestellen wir gerne eine Käseplatte. Wine lovers must visit Maxim at Gormannstraße 25 – we also like ordering the cheese plate.

CEE CEE'S GUEST: STEPHANIE FRANZIUS

Wilmersdorf, Wedding, Wohlfühlblase. Das sind, grob gesagt, die Wohn-Stationen von Stephanie Franzius. Aufgewachsen im Emser-Kiez, wo sie jedes Geschäft kennt, fühlt die Modemacherin sich dem Westen noch immer sehr verbunden. Aber über den Umweg Manhattan-Wedding ist sie schließlich nach Prenzlauer Berg gezogen. In die „Wohlfühlblase", mit „einem sehr speziellen Querschnitt an Einwohnern", sagt sie und lacht. Aber das hat nichts mit sich Lustigmachen zu tun, denn Stephanie begegnet allem und jedem auf Augenhöhe. Sie ruht in sich, habe sich freigestrampelt. Von den Zwängen des Modesystems. Inzwischen macht sie nur noch eine Kollektion pro Jahr – mit langen Kleidern in wunderbar leuchtenden Farben und sphärischen Allover-Prints. Und vor allem mit großzügig geschnittenen Mänteln aus hochwertigen Wollstoffen. Reinschlüpfen und gewappnet sein. Nicht nur für den rauen Berliner Winter, auch für die alltäglichen Anstrengungen. Diesen entkommt sie aber regelmäßig bei Ausflügen ins Umland oder einer Runde Minigolf unter Schwarzlicht. Wilmersdorf, Wedding, and her comfort zone Prenzlauer Berg: Stephanie Franzius has spent her phases in life in these districts. Raised in a neighborhood called Emser Kiez in Wilmersdorf where she knows every single shop, the fashion designer still feels strongly connected to West Berlin. After a short stay in Manhattan she moved to Wedding only to leave again for Prenzlauer Berg – the place to be back then. Today the clubs are elsewhere and it's better known for the cafés – it's a "comfortable bubble" with a "specific resident profile," says Stephanie and laughs. But she isn't making fun of her fellow residents. What's remarkable about her is that she regards everyone as being on equal footing. She's deeply relaxed because she broke free from the constraints of the fashion industry. Nowadays she plays by her own rules and launches one collection per year: long dresses and oversized coats made from high-quality wool are her staple items. Slip in and you are ready to go. Her coats are not only perfect for rough Berlin winters but also for dealing with daily challenges. Stephanie manages to escape them successfully – for example by playing black light miniture golf. →

franzius.eu
Franzius Shop, Schwartzkopffstraße 16, 10115 Berlin-Mitte
Open when open & by appointment

STEPHANIE FRANZIUS EMPFIEHLT: SCHWARZLICHT MINIGOLF

STEPHANIE FRANZIUS RECOMMENDS: BLACK LIGHT MINIGOLF

Was kann man bei regnerisch-kaltem Wetter bloß machen? Vielleicht etwas drinnen, im Warmen? Mit leichtem Aktivitätsfaktor für Groß und Klein, etwas, dass das Gemüt mittels Farb- und Lichttherapie anregt? Was könnte das nur sein...? Minigolf unter Schwarzlicht natürlich! Ein Fest für die Sinne! Mitten im Görlitzer Park, in einer ehemaligen, riesigen Garage befindet sich die erste Indoor-Schwarzlicht-Minigolfanlage mit 3D-Effekt. Hier spielt man sich – mit leichtem 80er-Jahre-Disco-Retro-Faktor – in psychedelisch anmutenden Wüsten- und Mondlandschaften, Fantasiewelten und simulierten Unterwasserkulissen von Loch zu Loch. Im Erdgeschoss befindet sich das Parkcafé, wo es Getränke und Kuchen sowie einen Indoor-Spielbereich für Kleinkinder gibt. Das Ganze macht aber auch als Nightlife-Warm-up Spaß, denn am Wochenende hat die Halle bis Mitternacht geöffnet. What can one do in rainy, cold weather? Perhaps some indoor activity with something that energizes and brightens up your day with light and color therapy. What could that possibly be...? Black light Minigolf under a black light of course! In the middle of Görlitzer Park, located in a huge former garage, you'll find the one and only indoor black light minigolf course with 3D effects – a feast for your senses. If you don't mind a bit of kookiness, you can complete all holes: the setting is made of psychedelic desert, moonscape, fantasy worlds, and pseudo-underwater zones. At the Parkcafé on the ground floor, they offer cakes and drinks and even an arcade zone for little children. The whole experience is a nice pre-party warm up activity as well. The hall is open until midnight on weekends.

Text: Stephanie Franzius / Photos: Sasha Kharchenko

Schwarzlicht Minigolf
Görlitzer Straße 1, Görlitzer Park, House No.1, 10997 Berlin-Kreuzberg
Mon-Thu 12:00-22:00, Fri 12:00-24:00, Sat 10:00-24:00, Sun 10:00-22:00
indoor-minigolf-berlin.de

Beim Paddeln in Burg im Spreewald findet Stephanie Ausgleich zur Atelierarbeit. Rowing in the Spreewald near Burg, is where Stephanie finds her balance after working hard in the studio.

MITTERNACHTSFRÜHSTÜCK UND AFTER HOUR-HANGOUT ALL DAY BREAKFAST, LATE NIGHT HANGOUT

Ein grellbunter Papagei aus Leuchtstoffröhren im Fenster, ein eingelassenes Pentagramm vor der Eingangschwelle. Das Schwarze Café ist ein Relikt aus der alten Welt, der ehemaligen Berliner City-West. Als Tages- und Nachtcafé ist es 24 Stunden geöffnet und bietet seinen Gästen ein unvergleichliches Flair – mit stuckbesetzten, hohen Räumen, gemütlichem Mobiliar und dem originellen Roten Zimmer. Ob als Tourist, Student oder Liebespaar auf ein „frühes Frühstück" nachts um 2 Uhr oder einfach nur um extern zu arbeiten – das Schwarze Café ist seit 1978 der richtige Ort dafür. Hier gibt es den Café au Lait noch in der klassischen französischen Bol, die Tische sind weiß gedeckt – und das mit Schwarzlicht ausgestattete WC legendär. Davon aber mal abgesehen: zu empfehlen sind die schwarzen Tortellini mit Lachsfüllung in Hummersoße und der täglich frische Kuchen. A flamboyant parrot made of fluorescent lights sits in the window, and a pentagram adorns the floor as you enter: welcome to Schwarzes Café, the "black café." This place is a relic from the old days – the former West Berlin. As a café that is open 24/7, it offers guests a unique flair: high traditional ceilings, walls decorated with stucco, cozy furniture, and its original red room. Whether you're a student or a tourist, visiting as a couple or with a group of friends, Schwarzes Café has been the perfect place for an early 2 a.m. breakfast since 1978. These days it's also a great place to work on your laptop. The café au lait is still served in a traditional French bowl. Try their black tortellini filled with salmon in lobster sauce. The tables are covered in white tablecloths and the black lighting in the restroom has become legendary.

Text: Nadine Dinter / Photos: Nadine Dinter, Marta Greber

Schwarzes Café
Kantstraße 148, 10623 Berlin-Charlottenburg
Daily all day except on Tue between 3:00-10:00
schwarzescafe-berlin.de

PER
SPE
CTI
VES

AUS DER VOGELPERSPEKTIVE KANN MAN EINE STADT VERSTEHEN UND BAUMWIPFEL ERBLICKEN. ODER DURCHS FENSTER SEHEN UND NEUE WELTEN ENTDECKEN. A BIRD'S-EYE VIEW CAN BE THE BEST WAY TO UNDERSTAND A CITY. BUT WE DON'T ALWAYS WANT TO SEE THE FOREST, WE ALSO WANT TO SEE THE TREES!

NÄCHSTER HALT: CAFÉ PFOERTNER
NEXT STOP: CAFÉ PFOERTNER

Ich sitze in einem ausrangierten Linienbus und schaue auf Industriewerkstätten – überall roter Klinker und eine überdimensionierte Toreinfahrt: Auf dem Gelände der ehemaligen BVG-Werkstätten ist ein Kulturzentrum entstanden, und in dem früheren Pförtnerhäuschen kann man heutzutage entspannt und gut essen. Mein persönlicher Tipp: zum Frühstück Müsli und abends lokales Bier zur hervorragenden Käseplatte. I'm sitting in a discarded public bus with a view of industrial workshops. I see brick walls everywhere, a parking lot, and an oversized entranceway. A former workshop of Berlin's public transportation company has been transformed into a cultural center; what was once a small house for the gatekeeper to monitor incoming vehicles has become a relaxing place for good food. I'd love to stay here all day and try everything from their daily menu. My personal tip: order muesli for breakfast and then come back in the evening with friends for some local beer and the superb cheese platter.

Text & photos: Martin Mascheski

Café Pförtner
Uferstraße 8-11, 13357 Berlin-Wedding
Breakfast: Mon-Fri 9:00-11:00, Sat 11:00-15:30; Lunch: Mon-Sat 12:00-15:30
Dinner: Mon-Sat 18:30-23:00
pfoertner.co

Kantinenessen mit fantastischem Panoramablick: die TU-Mensa im 20. Stock am Ernst-Reuter-Platz 7 in Charlottenburg. The University of Technology at Ernst-Reuter-Platz 7 has a cafeteria with a fantastic view from the 20th floor in Charlottenburg.

SUNDOWNER AUF DEM PARKHAUSDECK PARKING LOT ROOFTOP SUNDOWNER

Ich versuche von der Straße einen Blick aufs Dach der Neukölln Arcaden zu erhaschen, doch das Einkaufszentrum ist dafür zu hoch. Also steige ich in den Aufzug. Auch andere tun das, aber bald sind wir nur noch zu dritt und die Fahrt in die fünfte Etage bekommt etwas Konspiratives. Als sich die Türen oben öffnen, dämmert es gerade und Lichter leuchten von den Straßen herauf. Ich überquere das Parkhausdeck und gehe über die Autoauffahrt aufs Dach. Hier erwartet mich ein wunderbarer Blick über Neuköllns Dächer und eine selbst gezimmerte Sitzlandschaft. An der Bar kann man Cocktails bestellen, die Küche bereitet Piadine (italienisches Fladenbrot) zu und die Sonnenuntergänge werden jeden Abend musikalisch untermalt. Aber auch Frühaufstehern ist der Klunkerkranich zu empfehlen: ab 10 Uhr gibt's Frühstück. I try to catch a glimpse of the rooftop of the Neukölln Arcaden, but it is too high to see. I walk further to the shopping mall's entrance on Karl-Marx-Straße, and hop into a crowded garage elevator. After the 4th floor, only a few of us remain, and the whole place starts to feel a bit like a conspiracy. As the doors open on the 5th floor, I notice that lights are starting to illuminate on the top floor as dusk approaches. I walk across the empty parking lot and head to the ramp that takes me up to the rooftop. I enjoy the great view over the roofs of Neukölln and take a seat on the wooden improvised seating in the lounge area. Cocktails and piadina (Italian flatbread) are being served. Those who wish to enjoy the summer atmosphere can go for sunset drinks here every night. Those who wish to enjoy the summer atmosphere can go for sunset drinks here every night. The music's great too! For early birds: breakfast is served from 10 a.m.

Text: Lorena Simmel / **Photos:** Marta Greber

Klunkerkranich
Karl-Marx-Straße 66, 12053 Berlin-Neukölln
Mon-Sat 10:00-24:00, Sun 12:00-24:00

Wer pure Aussicht ohne Party sucht, steigt mittwochs oder freitags auf den Rathausturm Neukölln in der Karl-Marx-Straße 83. Die genauen Öffnungszeiten findet man auf berlin.de. If you prefer the view of Neukölln without cocktails: Neukölln's city hall tower (Rathausturm) at Karl-Marx-Straße 83 is open to visitors on Wednesdays and Fridays. The exact times are published on berlin.de

Bar

KUNST AM WASSER — EIN NACHMITTAG AM WALDSEE

HAUS AM WALDSEE — ART & CULTURE ON THE LAKE

In Anbetracht des überfüllten Freibads Plötzensee oder der raren Liegeplätze am Schlachten- und Tegeler See, hätte man schon fast Lust, den Ausflug an den Stadtsee abzuhaken - aber Stopp: Es gibt noch den Waldsee, ein Geheimtipp in Zehlendorf. Eigentlich als Privatsee für die umliegenden Villen gedacht, findet man hier auch als Normalsterblicher seinen Platz am Ufer: beim Haus am Waldsee. Bereits 1946 als Ausstellungshaus gegründet, wird heute zeitgenössische Kunst von Berliner Bildhauern, Malern und Fotografen gezeigt. Neben dem Café mit Minigolfbahn im Skulpturengarten gibt es auch einen direkten Zugang zum Wasser. After seeing how overcrowded Plötzensee's lido, Tegeler lake and Schlachten Lake get during summertime, you've probably decided to give up on city lakes altogether. Hold on. Try Wald Lake (Waldsee), hidden in the middle of Zehlendorf. Although it's mainly a private lake for surrounding villas, you still always manage to find a good spot by the shore near the Haus am Waldsee, a contemporary art exhibition space. While you're there, make sure to visit the miniature golf course and - of course - the current exhibition.

Text: Laura Storfner / Photos: Benjamin Lindenkreuz

Haus am Waldsee
Argentinische Allee 30, 14163 Berlin-Zehlendorf
Tue-Sun 11:00-18:00
hausamwaldsee.de

ZEITGENÖSSISCHES IM SCHINKEL PAVILLON
CONTEMPORARY ART AT SCHINKEL PAVILION

Früher traf man hier Erich Honecker zur Cocktailstunde, heute stößt die Kunstwelt im Schinkel Pavillon auf gelungene Vernissagen an. Der deutsche Architekt Richard Paulick erbaute das rundum verglaste Gebäude im Garten des Kronprinzen-palais im Jahr 1969; mittlerweile lädt Gastgeberin und Foto-künstlerin Nina Pohl in den ehemaligen SED-Parteitempel: Zeitgenössische Skulptur, Installation und Medienkunst locken die Besucher. Geheimtipps wie das Berliner Künstler-kollektiv Das Numen treffen auf große Namen wie Anselm Reyle, Isa Genzken und Camille Henrot. Wem es während der Eröffnungen zu voll wird, der geht auf die Terrasse und genießt die unverstellte Sicht auf Berlins Architekturperlen. More than 30 years ago Erich Honecker had cocktails at the Schinkel Pavilion. Today the art world clinks glasses here. German architect Richard Paulick built the all-glass house in the garden of the Crown Prince's Palace (Kronprinzenpalais) in 1969. Photo artist and host Nina Pohl still invites visitors to the former temple of the SED Party, but the audience and the occasions have changed. Today, contemporary sculpture, installation, and media art attract visitors. This is where the Berlin artist collective The Numen meets big names such as Anselm Reyle, Isa Genzken, and Camille Henrot. When the openings are packed, escape to the terrace and enjoy the unobstructed views of Berlin's architecture.

Text: Laura Storfner / Photos: Thorsten Klapsch

Schinkel Pavillon
Oberwallstraße 1, 10117 Berlin-Mitte
Thu-Sat 12:00-18:00
schinkelpavillon.de

DER GROSSSTADT-DSCHUNGEL AM ZOO INNER CITY JUNGLE BY THE ZOO

In den 1950er-Jahren war das Bikinihaus am Zoo das „Schaufenster des Westens“, heute soll es den Zoo als „Konsumterrain“ wiederbeleben. Untergebracht sind über 50 Geschäfte auf drei Etagen, gemeinsam bilden sie Deutschlands erste Concept-Mall. Der Leitsatz: kultureller Austausch in einer Lifestyle-Welt mag phrasenhaft klingen, sind doch auch große kommerzielle Namen wie Block House und Kaisers hier zu Hause. Aber vielleicht macht es die Mischung: Andreas Murkudis ist hier vertreten; Shops wie Odeeh und Supernova ergänzen das Konzept. Von der Terrasse aus blickt man direkt ins Affengehege; Paviane klettern, Papageien schreien - und dazwischen flaniert der Berliner. Back in the 1950s, Bikinihaus was grand. The building was "a window onto the West." Since its re-opening in 2014, it's become big again. Bikini Berlin is a shopping center near the Berlin Zoo. You'll find over 50 stores located on three floors in this so-called concept mall. Its slogan, "cultural exchange in a lifestyle world" might sound elitist, but you'll find big commercial names here too, like Block House and Kaiser's supermarket. It's a mix of low and high, mundane and exclusive. For example, Berlin's smartest shop owner Andreas Murkudis has installed another wonderful store here, and German fashion brand Odeeh joined as well. From the terrace, you can watch the monkeys running in their compound, the baboons and parrots screaming, and Berliners prancing around in this zoo of consumerism.

Text: Laura Storfner / Photos: Franz Brück

Bikini Berlin
Hardenbergplatz 2, 10623 Berlin-Charlottenburg
Mon-Sat 10:00-20:00
bikiniberlin.de

EIN HAUCH PARIS IM WESTEN
A CUP OF PARIS IN THE WEST

Eines unserer Lieblingscafés im Westen ist das Savigny. Der Schokoladenkuchen ist ein Traum und die Besitzerin hat einen exzellenten Geschmack in Sachen Zeitschriften und Zeitungen. Eine so große Auswahl an internationaler Presse sieht man in Berlin eher selten – da bestellt man gerne mal ein zweites oder drittes Getränk. Draußen in der Sonne fühlt man sich ein bisschen wie in Paris. Ein Muss, wenn man in der Gegend ist! Café Savigny is my favorite coffee shop in the West. Their rich chocolate cake is a dream come true and the owner has excellent taste in magazines and newspapers – such a large selection is rare for a café in Berlin. So beware – you may find yourself unwittingly ordering a third round of drinks while reading foreign papers in the sun. It can easily give you the illusion of sitting in a café in Paris. A must if you're in the area!

Text: Sven Hausherr / Photos: Sasha Kharchenko

Café Savigny
Grolmanstraße 53, 10623 Berlin-Charlottenburg
Daily 9:00-1:00

Delikate französische Backwaren zum Mitnehmen gibt es in der Pâtisserie Du Bonheur in der Brunnenstraße 39 in Mitte. Need your Paris fix? Head over to Pâtisserie Du Bonheur at Brunnenstraße 39 in Mitte and delve into their fine French pastries.

RAST MIT ZUGVÖGELN – ZUR KRANICHBEOBACHTUNG AUFS LAND AWE-INSPIRING CRANE VIEWING IN THE COUNTRYSIDE

Jedes Jahr von Ende September bis Anfang November findet ein einzigartiges Spektakel statt: Keilförmige Flugformationen aus Tausenden von Kranichen und anderen Zugvögeln überqueren Deutschland und ziehen gen Süden. Vor ihrem gemeinsamen Abflug legen sie noch einen Stopp an geeigneten Rastplätzen ein, um sich Energiereserven anzufressen. Wir fahren gerne in das Linumer Teichgebiet. Hier empfängt uns eine imposante Geräuschkulisse, und nicht nur auf dem See herrscht reges Treiben, auch auf den abgeernteten Maisfeldern stehen unzählige Vögel. Ein beeindruckendes Schauspiel - nicht nur für Ornithologen und Naturfreunde in Olivgrün. Every fall, a grand spectacle takes place in the surrounding areas of Berlin: thousands of cranes fly in an echelon migrating over Germany. Before the real flight begins, the birds stop at several locations to gas up and energize. One of these rest spots is Rügen in the Baltic Sea, but quite a few are located around Berlin too: Gülper Lake in the west of Berlin and Linum in the Fehrbellin area. As we hit the road northbound to Linum's pond area (Linumer Teichgebiet), an overwhelming sound made by the migrating cranes welcome us. The nearby cornfields have become a temporary home for a vast number of cranes as well. Suddenly, we start to see the sky turn black near the horizon as migrating birds take flight in large flocks. What an impressive sight, not only for ornithologists and birdwatchers dressed up in green overalls but for everyone to experience.

Text: Milena Kalojanov / Photos: Rei Matsuoka

Linumer Teichgebiet
16833 Fehrbellin

KOENIG WILHELM I
ZUM GEDAECHTNISS

EIN AUSFLUG ZUM GRUNEWALD-TURM AN EXCURSION TO GRUNEWALD TOWER

Von diesem roten Backsteinturm aus bietet sich ein fantastischer Blick auf das ferne Stadtzentrum, den Teufelsberg und die Havel. Wenn man mit der S-Bahn bis „Grunewald“ fährt und vom Schmetterlingsplatz aus startet, erreicht man den Turm in ungefähr eineinhalb Stunden. Zurück kann man den Bus nehmen, der direkt davor abfährt. Ein idealer Kurztrip für alle, die beim Waldspaziergang gerne ein Ziel vor Augen haben. Going up the red brick Grunewald Tower is a great, relaxing experience. From here, you have a fantastic view of the surrounding forests, Teufelsberg Hill, the Havel River, and Berlin's city center. If you take the S-Bahn to "Grunewald" and start your walk from Schmetterlingsplatz, it takes about one and a half hours to get to the tower. It's an easy walk with small road signs along the path to guide you. It's the perfect trek if all you have is half a day. In the end, you will be rewarded with a beautiful view. For your way back, just hop on the bus, since it stops right in front of the tower.

Text: Nina Trippel / Photos: Andreas Alexander Bohlender

Grunewaldturm
Havelchaussee 61, 14193 Berlin-Grunewald

Eine Lichtung im Grunewald nahe des Teufelsees, die man nicht verpassen sollte: die Sandgrube – fast wie am Meer, nur ohne Wasser. Not to be missed: the sand dune in the Grunewald forest close to the Teufel Lake is like being on the beach – just without the water.

ACTIVITIES

BARS

CAFÉS

CULTURE

EVENTS

MISCELLANEOUS

RESTAURANTS

SHOPS

Im Jahr 2011 haben wir den ersten Newsletter mit unseren ganz persönlichen Empfehlungen an 208 Freunde versendet. Nach dreieinhalb Jahren ist der Donnerstag noch immer jede Woche für Cee Cee reserviert. Inzwischen haben sich rund 15.000 Abonnenten in unseren Verteiler eingetragen, und über die Jahre haben wir mit unserem großartigen Team mehr als 800 Tipps gesammelt. Grund genug, das Beste vom Besten als Buch zusammenzufassen: CEE CEE BERLIN enthält persönliche Lieblingsorte und jüngste Neuentdeckungen, gespickt mit den spannendsten Gastbeiträgen der letzten drei Jahre.

Einige Cafés und Restaurants werden vielleicht demnächst schon umgezogen sein oder neue Filialen eröffnet haben, andere bald nicht mehr existieren. Der viel zitierte Wandel Berlins ist kein Klischee, sondern ein fortwährendes Phänomen. Mit unserem wöchentlichen Newsletter versuchen wir, Schritt zu halten. Melde Dich an unter ceecee.cc und folge uns auf unseren zukünftigen Streifzügen durch die Stadt.

Aber Cee Cee ist nicht nur ein elektronischer Brief von uns für Dich: Erst die Tipps und Entdeckungen unserer Leser machen Cee Cee zu einem authentischen und überraschenden Wegweiser. In diesem Sinne: Verrate uns Deine Neuentdeckungen und Lieblingsorte. Wir freuen uns über Input und Vorschläge, damit wir dieses Projekt gemeinsam noch weiter wachsen lassen können.

We'll Cee Cee you.
Xoxo

It all started in April 2011 – we sent our first newsletter with personal recommendations to 208 friends. Three and a half years later, every Thursday is still Cee Cee day for us. Meanwhile, we have grown to over 15,000 subscribers, and together with our amazing team we've created an archive of more than 800 Berlin-related tips. The time has come to compile and turn our "best of" into a book: CEE CEE BERLIN. This book includes many of our personal favorites along with some of the most exciting guest contributions from the past, sprinkled with new recommendations.

In the near future, some cafés, stores, or venues might move to new locations, open new branches, or fold their business; Berlin is a city of change – and it's not a cliché. Keeping up with the fast pace of this city can be a challenge. Subscribe to the newsletter on ceecee.cc and we'll send you our selection of not-to-be-missed information in and around Berlin: once a week, directly into your inbox.

But remember, Cee Cee is not exclusively made by us for you; your readership and contributions play a big role in making it truly Berlin. Please keep sharing stories of your favorite local spots and other recommendations by sending us an email.

We'll Cee Cee you.
Xoxo

Danke an alle bisherigen Gastautoren, die
Cee Cee seit 2011 jede Woche
bereichert haben Thanks to all of our guest contributors
who have enriched Cee Cee since 2011

Aida Baghernejad / Ailine Liefeld / Alex Rütten / Alexander Schierl
Alice Kuhn / Alma Clausen / Amanda Herman Tischbier
Ana Nuria Schmidt / Ana Santos / Anastazja Moser / Anders Ehlin
André M. Wyst / Angie Ziehmann / Anja Kunack / Anna Berge
Anna Russ / Anna Winger / Anna-Maria Scharf / Anne Jost
Anne Postrach / Antje Drinkuth / Ari Stein / Ariel Schlesinger
Arthur Groeneveld / Ashley Ludaescher / Astrid Bruckmann
Barbara Russ / Bettina Krieg / Carlito Schilirò / Caroline Wegener
Celina Plag / Christiane Kreisel-Büstgens / Christina Hartmann
Christina Müller / Clare Freeman / Claudia Charlotte Richstein
Daniel Wang / Deniz Julia Güngör / Despina Stokou
Diane Bergmann / Dirk Mönkemöller / Elena Podlubnaja
Elin S. Kann / Elisabeth Schotte / Ettina Berrios-Negrón
Eugenie Schmidt / Eva Kaczor / Fenke Gabriel-Schwan
Feride Uslu / Florian Storm / Frank Scrock / Gisela Williams
Hanna Rix / Helena Franke / Hendrik Borgmann / Henrik Mauler
Hien Le / Isa Griese / Jakob Braeuer / James Castle / Jamie Raap
Jana Gioia Baurmann / Janine Sack / Jana Gumprecht / Jenni Schmitt
Jeroen van Marle / Joanna Kalosoumi / Johanna Bardorz
Judith Peller / Juli Reinecke / Julica Norouzi / Karline Lisk
Katharina Beckmann / Katharina Gräfe / Katherine Sacks
Kavita Meelu / Kerstin Carl / Kirsten Hermann / Lisa Uduak
Lorena Simmel / Loris Haller / Lydia Willie / Magdalena Killinger
Maike Gossen / Maria Elisa Gerace / Marion Kadi / Martin Behnke
Mauro Paglia / Max Winter / Michael Müller / Nadine Dinter
Nadine El Ishmawi / Nadine May / Nele Heinevetter / Nella Beljan
Nell May / Nicky Aerts / Nicolas Kantor / Nikolaus Hurlbrink
Olga Blumhardt / Oliver Moore / Olivier Nowak / Pauline Hoch
Per Meurling / Philip Gaedicke / Philipp Reichel / Philippe Nowotny
Rosann Brandt / Rut Sigurðardóttir / Sabine Menzel
Sandra Diana Troegl / Sandra Tebbe / Sarah Weinknecht
Sharon Welzel / Sonja Stössel / Stefan Schuster / Stefanie Gerke
Stephan Deisenhofer / Stephanie Franzius / Suse Wittmann
Sven Giese / Sylee Gore / Tara Dominguez / Tessa Apitz
Tim Berge / Tim Seifert / Tutia Schaad / Verena Schwarz
Viviane Stappmanns / Yüksel Yilmaz

Ohne sie wäre Cee Cee in den letzten Jahren nicht möglich gewesen Without them Cee Cee would have not been possible

Rei Matsuoka / Laura Storfner / Milena Kalojanov

Das Konzept dieses Buches wurde in Zusammenarbeit entwickelt mit The concept of this book was conceived together with

Cedric Retzmann / Mathis Neuhaus / Laura Storfner
Max von Thadden / Jonas Vahl

Danke allen, die Cee Cee jede Woche möglich machen und wachsen lassen sowie jenen, die mitgeholfen haben, dieses Buch zu realisieren. Thanks to everyone involved in bringing Cee Cee to life week after week, and to the people who helped realize and develop this book

Alexander Trippel / Angelika Taschen / Amanda Herman Tischbier
Andreas Alexander Bohlender / Anna-Maria Scharf
Astrid Bruckmann / Beglu Karahan / Benjamin Lindenkreuz
Brigitte Trippel / Cathy Lara / Claudia Trippel / Christian Boros
Christin Berger / Christina Hartmann / Cedric Retzmann
Carlito Schilirò / Dominik Rompza / Eva Biringer / Frederik Kugler
Jalscha Römer / Johanna Bardorz / Jonas Vahl
Julia Michaelsen / Julien Braun / Lorena Simmel / Lydia Willie
Lynn Battaglia / Nella Beljan / Marta Greber / Martin Mascheski
Mathis Neuhaus / Max von Thadden / Michael Müller / Oliver Kann
Olivier Nowak / Pascal Rohé / Karolina Rosina / Olga Schlosser
Sarah Mie Nass / Sascha Bente / Sasha Kharchenko
Sharon Welzel / Sonja Bahr / Tobias Faisst / Uta Grosenick

Künstlerliste / List of artists

Cover

Manfred Pernice, AVA, Allgemeine Verkstatt Ausstellung, 2008 im / at Schinkel Pavillon

18

oben / top: Sarah Schönfeld
unten / bottom: Thomas Ruff

19

links / left, rechts / right: Elger Esser
Mitte / center: Thomas Ruff

23

Patrick Caulfield

28

links und rechts / left and right: Wolfgang Tillmans
mitte / middle: Günther Förg

29

oben / top: Raoul de Keyser,
unten / bottom: Günther Förg

68

oben / top: Marianne Brandt

69

oben / top: Architekten Walter Gropius, Alex Cvijanovic und Hans Bandel

unten / bottom: Sammlung des Bauhaus-Archiv / View of the Baushaus-Archive collection

80

Thomas Schütte

81

Georg Kolbe

104

Im Uhrzeigersinn / clockwise:
Kraupa-Tuskany Zeidler: Katja Novitskova

Autocenter: Tobias Hoffknecht, Oliver Osborne, Brent Wadden

Sprüth Magers: Robert Morris

Thomas Fischer: Marcel Frey

PSM: Ariel Reichman

VW (VeneKlasen/Werner): Michael Williams

Peres Projects: Alex Israel

192

unten / below: Sigmar Polke, Frank Stella

242

Igor Paasch

246

unten / bottom: Cerith Wyn Evans

247

oben / top: Klara Lidén

unten / bottom: Ai Weiwei

270

Mitte / center: Erik Steinbrecher

unten / bottom: Christodoulos Panayiotou

271

Werner Aisslinger

233

oben / top: Cosima von Bonin

unten / bottom: Sharon Lockhart

240

oben / top: Petrit Halilaj

unten / bottom: Florian Slotawa

241

Dan Graham, Nalbach + Nalbach

272

Senta Baldamus

Fotos / Photos

Cover

Im Uhrzeigersinn / clockwise:

The Barn Roastery: Benjamin Lindenkreuz

Prinzessinnengärten: Marco Clausen

Schinkel Pavillon: Gunter Lepkowski; Courtesy of Manfred Pernice, Galerie Neu, Berlin, und / and Schinkel Pavillon

18 / 19

Courtesy of Fotografiesammlung Arthur de Ganay

23

Courtesy of Between Bridges

50

Courtesy of Haus der Kulturen der Welt

74

Courtesy of Yorck Kinogruppe

80 / 81

Courtesy of Georg Kolbe Museum, Berlin

99

Chapter One: Antje Schröder

Five Elephant: Courtesy of Five Elephant

Café 9: Aina Estruch Perlas

Andraschko: Torben Hölke / HiPi

100

Im Uhrzeigersinn / clockwise:

Rosebudd: Diana Djeddi

Daniel's Eatery: Ailine Liefeld

Mother's Mother: Courtesy of Kavita Meelu

Brotzeit: Courtesy of Julia Stark

Speisenklub: Uli Kohl

Fortuna's Table: Courtesy of Suzy Fracassa

I eat you: Thang Dai

101

Infarm: Courtesy of Infarm, Indoor Urban Farming GmbH

Himmelbeet: Courtesy of Himmelbeet gemeinnützige GmbH

104

Im Uhrzeigersinn / clockwise:

Kraupa-Tuskany Zeidler: Hans-Georg Gaul, Courtesy of Kraupa-Tuskany Zeidler, Berlin

Autocenter: Markus Bachmann

Sprüth Magers: Courtesy of Sprüth Magers, Berlin

Thomas Fischer: Torben Höke, Courtesy of Galerie Thomas Fischer

PSM: Hans-Georg Gaul, Courtesy of Ariel Reichmann und / and PSM, Berlin

VW (VeneKlasen/Werner): courtesy of VW (VeneKlasen/ Werner), Berlin

Peres Projects: Courtesy of Bureau N

105

Gorki Apartments: Harry Weber

Modern Houseboat: Courtesy of Chris & Oliver Laugsch

Tautes Heim: Courtesy of Ben Buschfeld

Linnen: Rita Lino Feliciano

Hüttenpalast: Courtesy of Silke Lorenzen

Courtesy of Michelberger Hotel

115-117

Courtesy of Familie Cato

136

Courtesy of SaarowTherme

145

Courtesy of Staub Shop / Staub Studio

158 / 159

Courtesy of Thone Negrón

166 / 167

Courtesy of My Plus One / Clare Freeman

188

Courtesy of MDC Cosmetic

192

Courtesy of Sammlung Hoffmann

217

Courtesy of uslu airlines

240

oben / top: Courtesy of Petrit Halilaj; Chert, Berlin
unten / bottom: Courtesy of Uwe Walter; 4. Berlin Biennale / 4th Berlin Biennial, 2006

Backcover

Im Uhrzeigersinn / clockwise:

Stechlinsee: Milena Kalojanov

Café Pfoertner: Martin Mascheski

Food: Marta Greber

Klunkerkranich: Marta Greber

Herausgeber & Konzeption / Editor & Concept

Cee Cee
Sven Hausherr & Nina Trippel

Art Direktion / Art Direction

Sven Hausherr

Grafik Design / Graphic Design

Studio Hausherr: Julien Braun, Benjamin Lindenkreuz, Julia Michaelsen, Karolina Rosina

Koordination / Coordination

Karolina Rosina

Redaktion deutsch / Co-Editing German

Laura Storfner

Redaktion english / Co-Editing English

Rei Matsuoka

Redaktionsassistenz / Editorial Assistance

Eva Biringer, Lorena Simmel

Übersetzung Gasttexte / Translation guest texts

Sarah Mie Nass

Lektorat Deutsch / Copy Editing German

DISTANZ Verlag: Frederik Kugler

Lektorat Englisch / Copy Editing English

Cathy Lara, Amanda Herman Tischbier, Rei Matsuoka
DISTANZ Verlag: Frederik Kugler, Lynn Battaglia

Vorwort / Foreword

Angelika Taschen

Autoren / Authors

Sascha Bente, Astrid Bruckmann, Nadine Dinter, Antje Drinkuth, Marta Greber, Kirsten Hermann, Nikolaus Hurlbrink, Milena Kalojanov, Ida Marie, Martin Mascheski, Rei Matsuoka, Oliver Moore, Mathis Neuhaus, Elena Podlubnaja, Juli Reinecke, Cedric Retzmann, Karolina Rosina, Tutia Schaad, Anna-Maria Scharf, Olga Schlosser, Lorena Simmel, Viviane Stappmanns, Laura Storfner, Max von Thadden, Claudia Trippel, Sarah Weinknecht, Lydia Willie, Max Winter

Gastautoren / Contributing Authors

Martin Behnke, Ettina Berrios-Negrón, BLESS, Stephanie Franzius, Jana Gumprecht, Kirsten Hermannn, Ailine Liefeld, Henrik Mauler, Ariel Schlesinger, Christian Schneider, Tim Seifert, Rut Sigurðardóttir

Porträtaufnahmen / Portrait Photography

Pascal Rohé

Stadtaufnahmen (Doppelseiten) / Street Photograpy (Spreads)

Andreas Alexander Bohlender

Fotografie / Photography

Andreas Alexander Bohlender, Gabriel Braun, Franz Brück, Kira Bunse, Thang Dai, Christine Davis, Emmanuel Decouard, Nadine Dinter, Diana Djeddi, Fred Dott, Edisonga, Fette Sans, Volker Eichenhofer, Aina Estruch Perlas, Tobias Faisst, Marta Greber, Ivo Gretener, Ira Hadžić, Mila Hacke, Loris Haller, Jan Nicolas Harting, Serge Hasenböhler, Achim Hatzius, Katja Hendlmayr, Karsten Hintz, Daniel Horn, Milena Kalojanov, Jan Kapitän, Sasha Kharchenko, Hartwig Klappert, Knut Klaßen, Uli Kohl, A.Kroth, Philipp Langenheim & Corina Schadendorf, Gunter Lepkowski, Ailine Liefeld, Benjamin Lindenkreuz, Jonas Lindström, Rita Lino Feliciano, Martin Mascheski, Peter Meffert, Julia Michaelsen, Noshe, Namy Nosratifard, Ludger Paffrath, Chloé Richard, Karolina Rosina, Ana Santl, Anna-Maria Scharf, Rachel Scheidt, Carlito Schilirò, Tim Schroeder, Miriam Siefert, Lothar Schnepf, Rut Sigurðardóttir, Hanna Skoog, Florian Wenningkamp, Uwe Walter, Robert Wunsch

Produktion / Production Management

DISTANZ Verlag, Sonja Bahr

Gesamtherstellung / Production

optimal media GmbH, Röbel/Müritz

© 2014 Cee Cee, die Autoren / the authors und / and Distanz Verlag GmbH, Berlin

Das Copyright für die abgebildeten Werke liegt bei den jeweiligen Künstlern außer / The copyright lies with the respective artist except

© VG Bild-Kunst, Bonn, 2014 für die abgebildeten Werke von / for the reproduced works by Hans Bandel, Marianne Brandt, Patrick Caulfield, Alex Cvijanovic, Elger Esser, Walter Gropius, Georg Kolbe, Robert Morris, Sigmar Polke, Thomas Ruff, Karin Sander, Thomas Schütte, Florian Slotawa, Erik Steinbrecher, Frank Stella

Vertrieb / Distribution

GESTALTEN, Berlin
www.gestalten.com
sales@gestalten.com

ISBN 978-3-95476-069-5
Printed in Germany

Erschienen im / Published by

DISTANZ Verlag
www.distanz.de

Kontakt / Contact

Cee Cee
Leipziger Straße 66
10119 Berlin-Mitte
www.ceecee.cc